PRESENTS

100% UNOFFICIAL

THE DEFINITIVE GUIDE TO
MINECRAFT
2026

A TOTALLY INDEPENDENT PUBLICATION

ISBN 978-1-917522-14-4

PILLAR BOX RED

Written by Naomi Berry
Designed by Adam Wilsher

WELCOME

WELCOME, EXPLORERS!
Get ready to jump back into the world of Minecraft we all know and love; where creepers are (always) creeping, diamonds are shining, the enderdragon is waiting, and your imagination can shape entire worlds.

It's been over **15** years since we've had Minecraft, and the game's greater than ever. With a massive movie dominating cinemas and record numbers of players on servers, it's clear the world of Minecraft is here to stay, and is showing no signs of slowing down. From deep in the mines or flying high above the clouds (courtesy of the game's latest update, Chase the Skies), it's clear to see that Minecraft just keeps getting bigger and better.

Whether you're a redstone expert (respect), a parkour legend, or someone who still starts every game by punching trees (no judgement, we've all been there), this book's packed with everything you need to navigate the unending world of blocks: pro tips, awesome builds, tricky puzzles, and plenty of Minecraft madness to keep things exciting.

We'll cover everything from the basics to the big stuff: home bases and mobs, commands to tinker with the game's innards and a few trips here and there to the Nether and the End.

So sharpen your sword, gather your supplies, and make sure you've set your respawn point - we might be out there for a while.

CONTENTS

GLOSSARY

MINECRAFT ISN'T JUST A GAME - IT'S A WHOLE UNIVERSE, FULL OF STRANGE LINGO AND QUIRKY MECHANICS THAT CAN LEAVE EVEN THE MOST EXPERIENCED BLOCK-BREAKERS SCRATCHING THEIR HEADS.

BEFORE YOU CHARGE INTO THE UNKNOWN - WHETHER IT'S LOOTING A VILLAGE, CRAWLING THROUGH CAVES, OR STUMBLING INTO A PORTAL FOR SOME CASUAL CROSS-DIMENSIONAL TRAVEL - IT MIGHT BE A GOOD IDEA TO BRUSH UP ON THE LANGUAGE OF THE GAME FIRST.

ADVENTURE

Adventure Mode is designed with player-made maps in mind. Instead of just trying to survive, this mode leans into storylines and set-challenges that give you a more structured way to play.

ALEX

Alex is one of the two default character models in Minecraft. She's the female counterpart to Steve, complete with slimmer arms and a ponytail.

AFK

Short for "away from keyboard." Not unique to Minecraft, but handy to know - it means the player's stepped away and isn't currently active.

BEDROCK

This is the bottom layer of the Minecraft world. If you've dug all the way down and hit bedrock, that's your stopping point; it's unbreakable in Survival mode.

BIOME

Biomes are different zones on the map, each with its own look, weather, and unique mobs or blocks to discover.

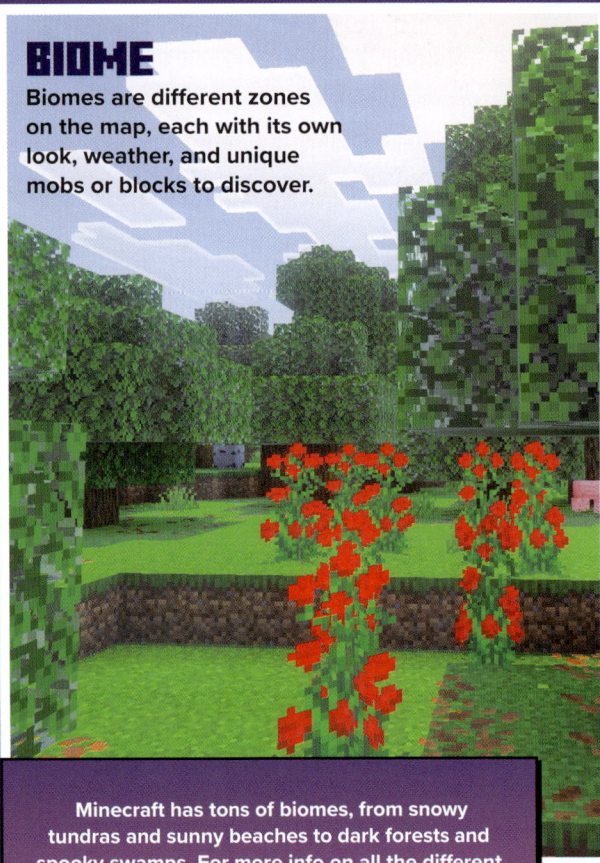

Minecraft has tons of biomes, from snowy tundras and sunny beaches to dark forests and spooky swamps. For more info on all the different types of biomes, check out the Biomes 101 chapter from p. 16-21.

BLOCK

Everything in Minecraft is made of blocks. These pixelated cubes are the building units of the whole game - terrain, structures, you name it.

BLOCK CLUTCH

A trick move where you save yourself from fall damage by placing a block under your feet just before you hit the ground. Skilled fingers only.

CAVING

When you're off exploring underground for resources, you're caving. Some cave systems get so big, they practically become their own adventure.

CHUNK

Short for "coordinates." These numbers track your exact location in the world and are super helpful for navigation.

COORDS

Shorthand for coordinates, these are used to note a specific position in the Minecraft world.

CRAFT

Crafting is central to everything in Minecraft. You combine materials to make tools, items, and structures - it's how you go from punching trees to building empires. For more on Crafting, check out p. 46-47.

CREATIVE

Creative Mode gives you unlimited resources and invincibility. Perfect for building, experimenting, or just goofing around without worrying about survival.

Game Mode: Creative

Do you know the differences between the game modes? In Survival, you collect resources and fight to stay alive. Creative gives you unlimited blocks so you can build anything. Adventure is for custom maps with stories and puzzles. Spectator lets you fly around and explore. Hardcore is like Survival but way tougher: one life, and it's game over!

CRIT

A critical hit does extra damage (1.5x more, to be exact). You can land one by striking while coming down from a jump.

DROP

Drops are items left behind after you break a block or defeat a mob. Collect them to use or craft later.

ELYTRA

The Elytra is a pair of rare wings that let you glide through the sky. You can only find them in End Cities, and they're a game-changer for travel.

ENCHANT

Enchanting boosts your gear with special effects, like extra damage or durability. It's a late-game mechanic, but super useful once you're geared up.

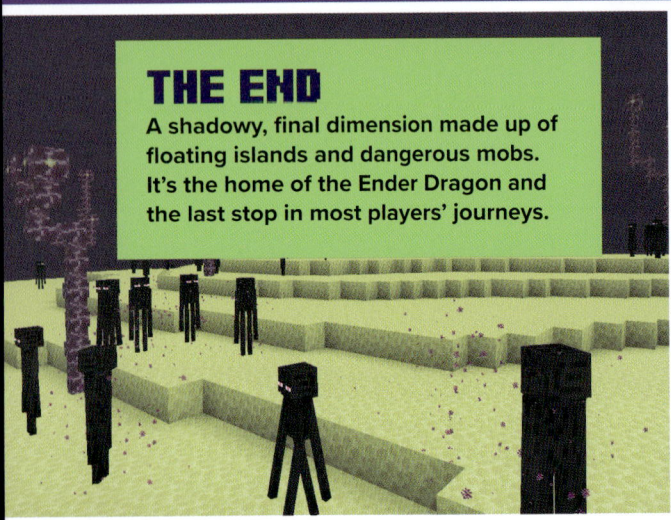

THE END

A shadowy, final dimension made up of floating islands and dangerous mobs. It's the home of the Ender Dragon and the last stop in most players' journeys.

ENDERMAN

Tall, spooky mobs that teleport and hate being looked at. Attack one, and get ready for a fight.

ENDER DRAGON

Minecraft's unofficial final boss. This giant flying mob lives in The End and takes some serious prep to defeat

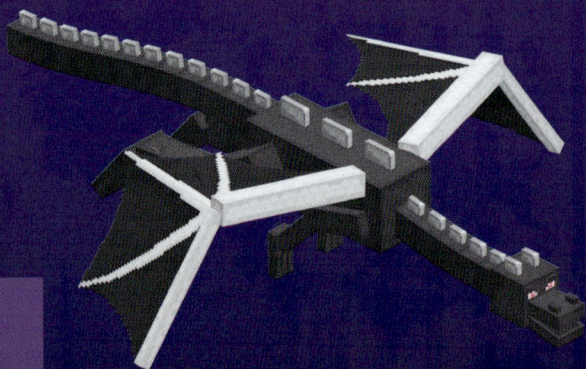

FIRE RES

Fire Resistance. A potion effect that makes you immune to fire and lava (absolutely essential in the Nether).

HARDCORE

Hardcore Mode is Survival with permadeath. One life only. If you die, your world gets deleted. Not for the faint of heart.

Game Mode: Hardcore

HOTBAR

The row of nine slots at the bottom of your screen. It's where you keep your go-to tools and items for quick access.

HOTKEY

Quick-switching items in your hotbar using keyboard shortcuts. It takes practice, but once you've nailed it, you'll play way faster.

INVIS

Short for Invisibility Potion. Makes you invisible to mobs and players (just don't forget your armour still shows!).

MLG

Short for "Major League Gaming," but used in Minecraft to mean pulling off a high-skill move, like clutch water-bucketing to avoid fall damage.

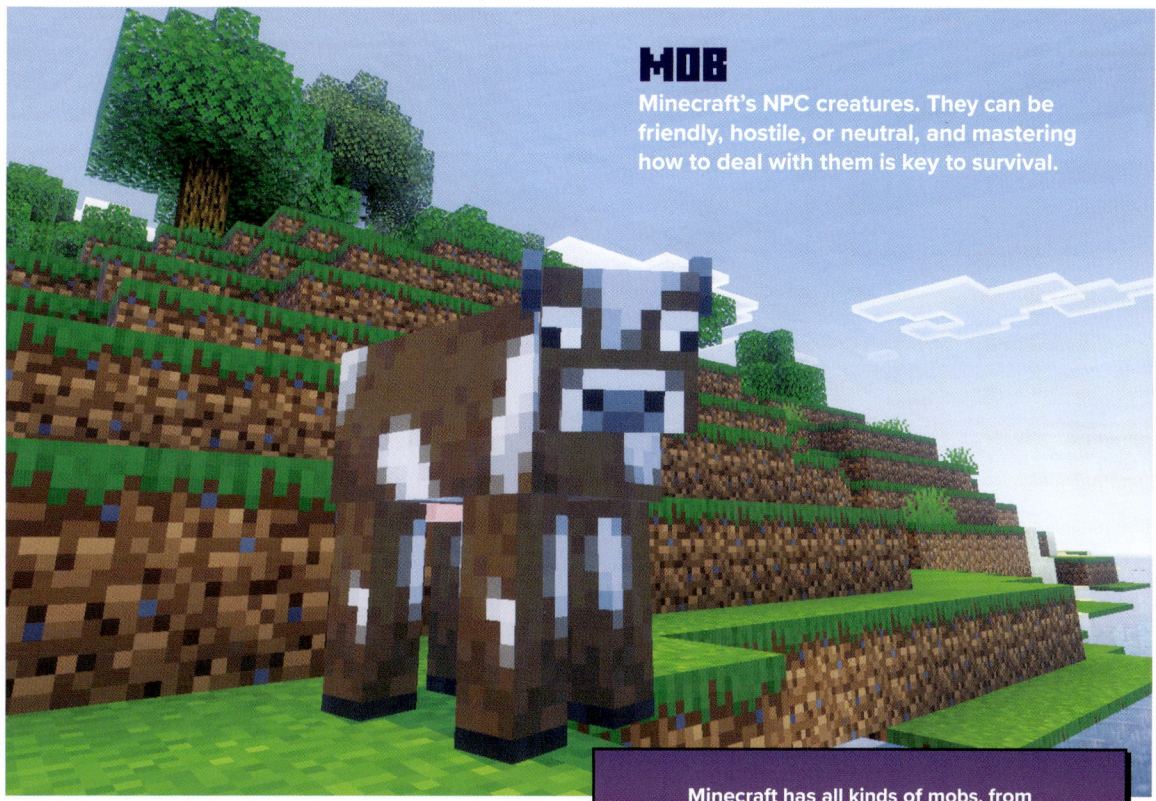

MOB

Minecraft's NPC creatures. They can be friendly, hostile, or neutral, and mastering how to deal with them is key to survival.

Minecraft has all kinds of mobs, from friendly animals like cows and sheep to scary ones like zombies and creepers. Some mobs help you out, some drop useful loot, and others just try to blow you up. Check out Minecraft Mobs on p. 28-31 for more info.

MOD

Mods are fan-made changes to the game that add new features, tweak gameplay, or totally transform the experience. Use with caution.

MOJANG

The studio behind Minecraft. Without Mojang, we'd all be living in a world without Creepers.

PICKAXE

One of the most important tools in the game. You need it to mine stone and ores, and the better the material, the faster it works.

NETHER

Minecraft's fiery underworld, packed with danger and valuable resources. Enter through a portal, but be ready to fight for your life.

Interdimensional travel piquing your interest? Check out p. 14-15 for more information on the three dimensions of Minecraft.

OVERWORLD

The main Minecraft dimension where you start your journey. It's full of biomes to explore and resources to gather.

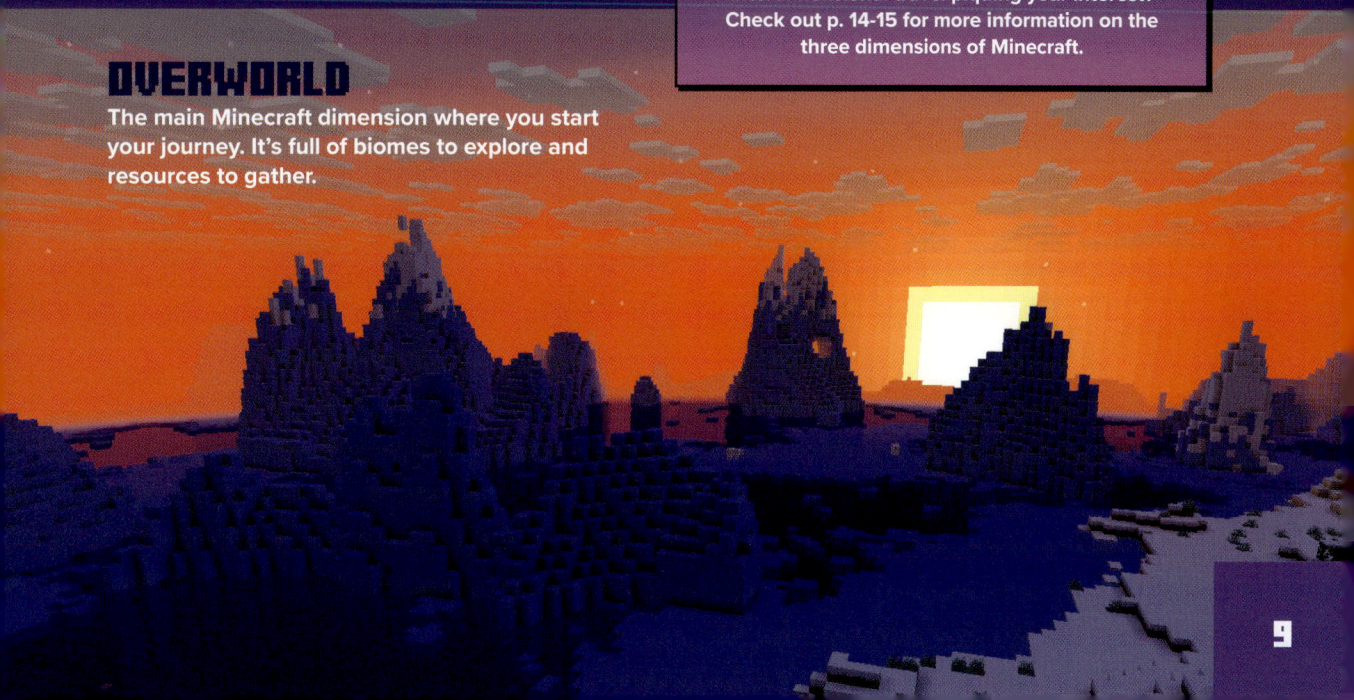

PORTAL

The only way to travel between dimensions. Build a Nether portal with obsidian; find and activate an End portal to reach the End.

PROT

Short for Protection, an enchantment that boosts your armour's defense stats.

PVE/PVP

Player vs. Environment (PvE) means fighting mobs and the world itself. Player vs. Player (PvP) is all about battling other players.

RNG

Random Number Generator. This is the system behind everything from loot drops to mob spawns. "Good RNG" means lucky. "Bad RNG" means... not so lucky.

SANDBOX

A type of game with no fixed goals. In sandbox mode, you set the rules and make your own fun.

Looking for other Sandbox games to play? Check out Boundless (Wonderstruck Games), Creativerse (Playful Studios), Dragon Quest Builders 2 (Square Enix), Lego Worlds (TT Games) or Terraria (Re-Logic).

SEED

A unique code that generates a Minecraft world. Sharing seeds lets players explore the same world layout.

SERVER

An online multiplayer world where players gather to explore, build, and compete together.

SKELLY

Minecraft slang for skeleton mobs. They shoot arrows and love lurking in dark corners.

SKIN

Your character's appearance. Steve and Alex are the defaults, but you can customize your look with different skins.

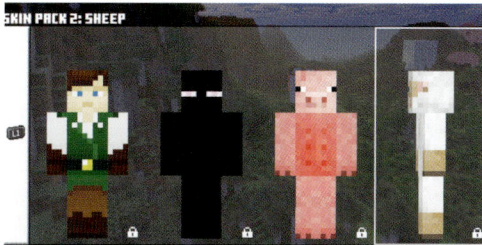

SPAWN

Your starting location in the world. If you die without setting a respawn point, you'll return to this default spot.

SPECTATOR

A game mode that lets you fly through the world without interacting. Great for scouting or watching others play.

STACK

Grouping identical items in your inventory, usually up to 64 per stack. Stacks save space and keep things tidy

SURVIVAL

The classic Minecraft experience. Gather, build, and survive as long as possible while managing hunger, health, and hostile mobs.

VANILLA

The unmodded version of Minecraft, pure and simple. If you're playing Vanilla, you're playing the game exactly as Mojang made it.

WITHER

Another boss-level enemy. The Wither is summoned using soul sand and wither skeleton skulls. It's destructive, aggressive, and not to be taken lightly - but defeating it will give you the super rare Nether Star.

XP

Experience Points. Earned through mining, fighting, breeding, and more. You'll need XP for enchanting and repairing gear.

STEVE

The original Minecraft character skin. Steve is the default player character and has been around since the very start of the game. Despite not being able to talk, he's become one of the most iconic and recognisable characters in all of gaming history.

MINECRAFT TIMELINE

FROM A TINY TEST WORLD TO A MEGA GLOBAL SENSATION, HERE'S HOW MINECRAFT TOOK OVER OUR SCREENS, ONE BLOCK AT A TIME!

2009

THE BEGINNING
The very first Minecraft version drops on May 17! It's just called Cave Game at first. It's super simple - but guess what? Players love it. Oh, and the Creeper? Total accident. But it stays... and starts blowing things up.

THE REALMS EXPAND
Spooky lava world? Don't mind if we do. The Nether arrives, and with it comes fire, zombie pigmen, and those screaming ghost-things called Ghasts. Oh, and fishing becomes a thing. Balance.

2010

2011

THE END BEGINS
Minecraft officially launches with The End, a creepy void dimension with the Ender Dragon as the final boss. Plus: XP, hunger bars, and villages.

MICROSOFT MOVES
Microsoft buys Minecraft for a gazillion dollars (okay, $2.5 billion, but close enough), which means Mojang officially joins the Microsoft squad, with full access to Microsoft's resources... but still keeping it indie at heart.

2014

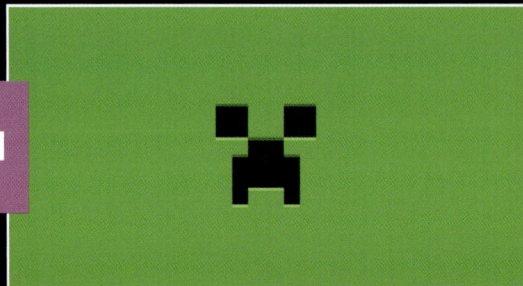

MINECRAFT GOES SWIMMING

Oceans get a massive glow-up, with dolphins, shipwrecks, treasure maps and tridents. The world expands twofold (threefold, even); deep sea diving opening up a whole new world (pun intended).

2018

THE NETHER BEEFS UP

The Nether gets new biomes (hello, warped forest), scary mobs like Piglins, and netherite gear - see ya, diamonds, it's been real.

2020

CAVES AND CLIFFS

The biggest world expansion since oceans, Caves and Cliffs expanded the explorable Y axis coordinates allll the way up and allll the way down. We can now scale cliff sides and mountains and dive deep down into dark caverns to discover new treasures, creatures and crawlies.

2021

IT'S STORYTIME

Archaeology, camels, and pink cherry blossom trees! This update adds storytelling vibes, and also sniffer mobs that sniff out ancient treasure. Adorable and useful.

2023

THINGS GET TRICKY

Who's ready for a challenge? Trial Chambers bring puzzles and traps, adding a little Indiana Jones adventure vibes to your usual cave expeditions.

2024

TO THE SKY!

The newest update brings us sky adventures, the Happy Ghast (yes, really), and the Player Locator Bar (so you finally stop getting lost).

2025

THE THREE DIMENSIONS

IN MINECRAFT YOU DON'T JUST EXPLORE ONE WORLD - YOU CONQUER THREE! EACH DIMENSION OFFERS UNIQUE LANDSCAPES, CREATURES, AND CHALLENGES - FROM BUILDING YOUR FIRST HOME AND TREASURE HUNTING IN HAUNTED SHIPWRECKS TO STAVING OFF HUNGER IN THE DEPTHS OF HELL AND TAKING ON DEMONIC DRAGONS. LET'S JOURNEY THROUGH THE OVERWORLD, THE NETHER AND (GULP) THE END.

THE OVERWORLD

The Overworld is your starting point in Minecraft. It features a massive variety of biomes including forests, deserts, oceans, jungles, caves and mountains. Villages, temples and ruins are scattered throughout the world, just waiting to be discovered. You'll find animals to farm, mobs to battle, and all the essential materials for crafting tools, weapons and armour.

This is the dimension where players spend most of their time. It is perfect for building bases, gathering resources and preparing for the dangers that lie beyond. Almost everything in Minecraft begins in the Overworld, from your first wooden pickaxe to your first enchanted netherite sword.

Tip! Keep a bed and respawn point ready before embarking on any interdimensional travel (just not in the Nether or the End - unless you like explosions interrupting your slumber).

THE NETHER

The Nether is a chaotic dimension packed with fireballs, lava lakes, and one deadly surprise: beds that explode when you try to sleep.

It's home to exclusive resources like nether quartz, netherite, blaze rods and warped wood. You'll also find Nether Fortresses and Bastion Remnants, massive structures packed with loot and tough enemies like blazes, wither skeletons and piglin brutes.

You'll need to build a Nether Portal if you want to head into the Nether. You'll need obsidian blocks arranged in a rectangular frame (at least 4x5). Light the portal using flint and steel, and step in to arrive in the Nether. It's an immediate journey, so make sure you're well equipped before you go.

A unique feature of the Nether is that distances work differently. One block moved in the Nether equals eight blocks in the Overworld, making it a great way to travel long distances quickly by building linked portals.

It's a good idea to always bring gold gear into the Nether to avoid being attacked by piglins.

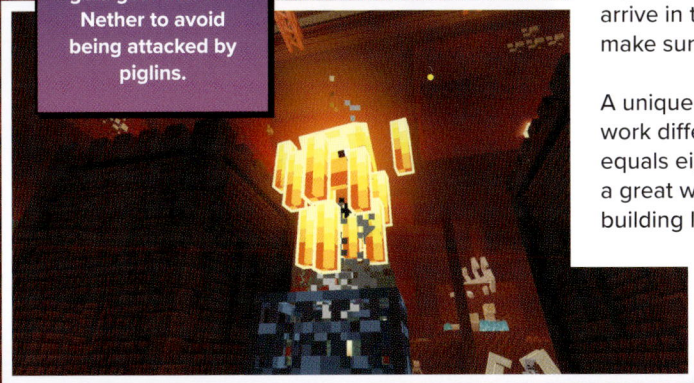

THE END

If the Nether feels like danger turned up to eleven, the End is something even stranger: a shadowy, silent world that feels like a waking nightmare. This otherworldly dimension is made up of floating islands above an endless void, and is home to Minecraft's final boss and toughest enemy, the ender dragon.

After defeating the dragon, you'll unlock a portal that leads to the outer End islands, where you can find End Cities and Ships. These structures hold some of the rarest and most valuable items in the game, including Elytra (wings that let you glide) and shulker boxes (storage that keeps items when broken).

To reach the End, you'll need to find an End Portal within a stronghold in the Overworld - but they're not easy to find; you'll need a good supply of eyes of ender and plenty of patience. Once you find a portal, fill it with the eyes of ender to activate it.

The End is a dangerous place, with limited resources and no easy way out. Come prepared, build bridges, and always watch your step.

Not trying to trigger any endermen attacks? Wear a carved pumpkin on your head to avoid angering any of them.

BIOMES 101

WHEN YOU STEP INTO A NEW MINECRAFT WORLD, THE FIRST THING YOU NOTICE ISN'T JUST THE BLOCKS - IT'S THE VIBE OF THE PLACE. THAT VIBE? THAT'S THE BIOME.

BIOMES ARE REGIONS WITH THEIR OWN LOOK, CLIMATE, WILDLIFE, AND RESOURCES. THEY SHAPE HOW YOU PLAY, WHAT YOU BUILD, WHAT YOU FIND, AND WHAT KIND OF MOBS YOU'LL RUN INTO. SOME ARE CALM AND SAFE, PERFECT FOR SETTING UP BASE AND BUILDING YOUR DREAM HOME. OTHERS? NOT SO MUCH.

OVERWORLD BIOMES

PLAINS

Plains are some of the most common biomes in Minecraft. They stretch out with flat, open ground, green grass and the occasional oak tree for variety. Plains are peaceful biomes, perfect for spotting sheep, cows, pigs, and sometimes even the odd horse or mule grazing nearby. Oh, and if you're lucky, you might stumble across a village nestled among the fields that's prime for pillaging. Or peaceful cohabitation. But probably pillaging.

What makes the plains especially popular is how easy they are to build on. The level terrain means you don't have to do much digging or terraforming to start crafting your dream base. And want to add a splash of colour? The wildflowers that grow here are perfect for decorating your builds or crafting dyes.

BIOMES

Plains, Ice Plains, Ice Spike Plains, Sunflower Plains, Snowy Plains, Mushroom Field, Savanna

WOODLANDS

Woodland biomes are full of life, color, and trees. Lots and lots of trees. From the bright birch forests to the shadowy depths of the dark forest, each forest brings its own mood and resources. Whether you're after wood, wildlife, or the perfect hidden base, there's always something waiting beneath the trees.

The pale garden is one of the newest biomes in Minecraft. It's a rare forest biome filled with pale oak trees (the only place they grow in the game) and the creepiest new hostile mob: creakings.

BIOMES

Forest, Birch Forest, Dark Forest, Flower Forest, Old Growth Birch Forest, Taiga, Old Growth Spruce Taiga, Old Growth Pine Taiga, Snowy Taiga, Jungle, Bamboo Jungle, Sparse Jungle, Grove, Cherry Grove, Pale Garden

CAVES

Cave biomes turn the underground into a whole new adventure. Lush caves are full of moss, vines, and glowing berries, with axolotls splashing in the water and roots hanging from the ceiling. Dripstone caves are spiky and dramatic, with giant stone formations that can fall on your head, so tread carefully.

But the deepest and darkest (and scariest) is the deep dark. It's silent, creepy, and pitch black - trigger a sculk sensor and it'll summon a warden, and trust: you do not want to meet that unprepared. Still, if you're quiet (and lucky), you could find ancient cities packed with rare loot and mysterious blocks.

BIOMES

Deep Dark, Dripstone Caves, Lush Caves

Things can get dark and dangerous fast, so it's safest to explore caves with your coordinates turned on. On desktop, press F3 to open the debug menu and see your coordinates. On console, just check your map to find them.

MOUNTAINS

Mountain biomes bring the drama all the way up on the Y-axis, with towering cliffs, deep valleys, and some of the best pixelated views in the game. If you're looking to build high above the clouds (or go goat-spotting), then this is the place to do it.

Lower down, things get a little calmer. Meadows are peaceful grassy plateaus with flowers, bees, and the occasional lone tree. Windswept hills and forests are rugged and uneven, full of surprises and great for adventurous builds.

BIOMES

Jagged Peaks, Frozen Peaks, Stony Peaks, Snowy Slopes, Windswept Hills, Windswept Forest, Windswept Gravelly Hills, Meadow, Stony Shores, Savanna Plateau, Windswept Savanna

BIOMES

Swamp, Mangrove Swamp

SWAMPS

Swamps are mysterious, muddy places full of thick trees, hanging vines, and lots of squishy mud. The classic swamp has murky water, lily pads, and those spooky witch huts hiding in the shadows.

Mangrove Swamps are newer and even wetter, with tangled roots rising out of the water and new blocks like mud to dig up. You'll want a boat to explore here, and if you're lucky, you might spot some frogs hopping through the reeds.

> Keep an eye out for slimes hopping around at night in swamps; they're perfect for slimeball fans and redstone builders.

SANDY AREAS

Sandy biomes bring the heat and the color, from sunbaked deserts to the layered cliffs of the Badlands. Deserts are dry and dusty, filled with cacti, temples, and husks that never sleep. Beaches offer a chill spot between land and water, where you can catch fish or build a seaside base (beachfront properties are always in).

Badlands are easy to spot due to their intense colours (thanks terracotta), and the best spot for mining for gold. The wooded and eroded badlands have trees and jagged cliffs to the terracotta landscapes.

BIOMES

Badlands, Wooded Badlands, Eroded Badlands, Beach, Snowy Beach, Desert

WATER AREAS

Around 25-33% of the Overworld's surface is ocean, so it makes sense that there are a whole lot of different water biomes. Rivers flow through the land, occasionally freezing over. Oceans stretch out forever, with coral reefs, dolphins, and hidden shipwrecks waiting to be discovered.

Frozen oceans are chilly and full of icebergs, while warm oceans glow with colorful fish and turtles. There's always something to discover below the surface in the Overworld.

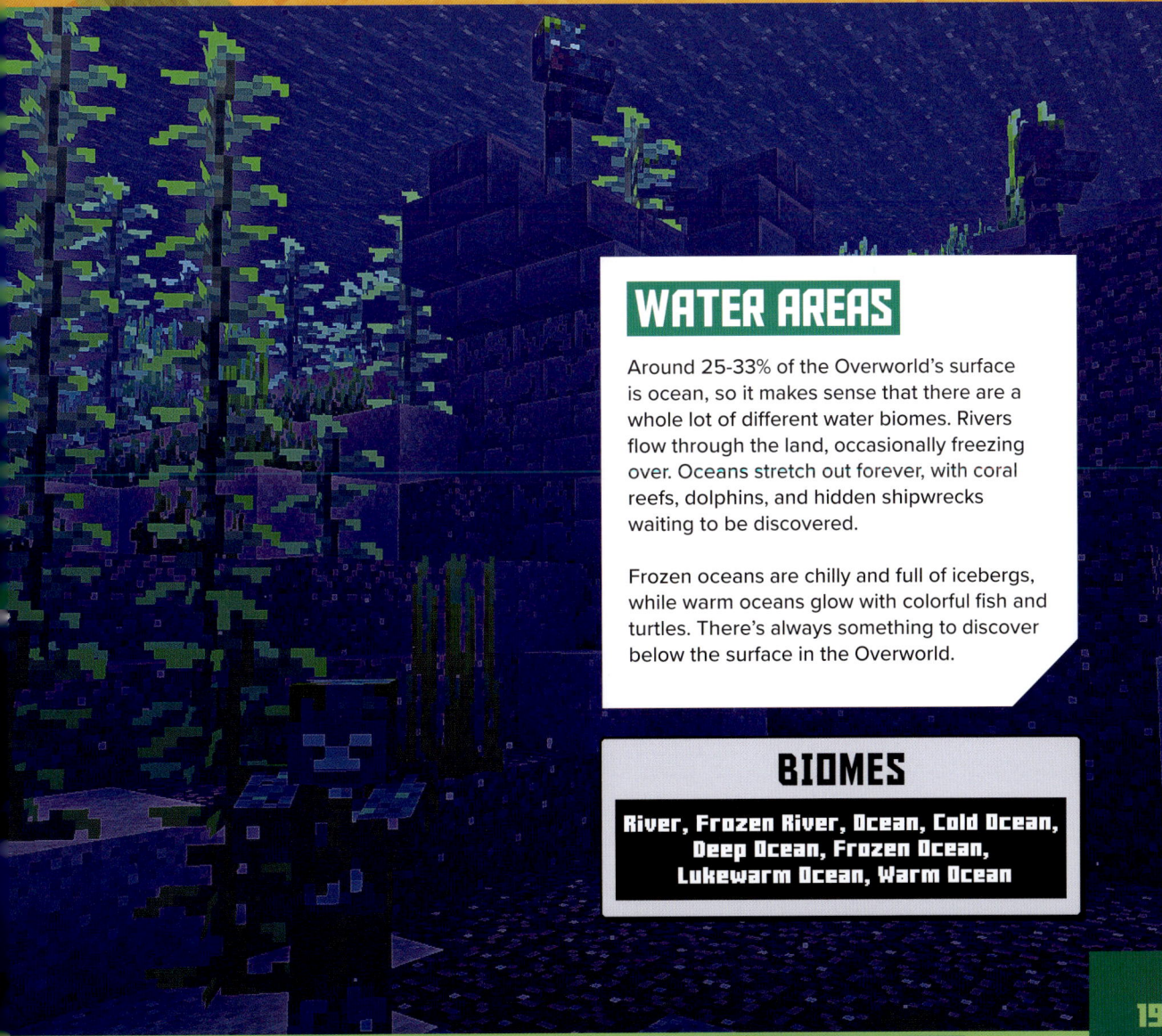

BIOMES

River, Frozen River, Ocean, Cold Ocean, Deep Ocean, Frozen Ocean, Lukewarm Ocean, Warm Ocean

NETHER BIOMES

The Nether is a wild, fiery dimension packed with strange landscapes and even stranger mobs. Not one of them is safe. Nether wastes are full of fire, lava lakes and ghasts. Soul sand valleys are eerie and quiet, swathed in blue fog and spooky soul sand that slows you down. Basalt deltas are volcanic nightmares with ash floating in the air. Crimson and warped forests are full of giant colourful fungi and classic Nether mobs like piglins and endermen.

The Nether is a place to test your courage - and your parkour skills.

The Nether is a tough place to navigate, but it's worth it for the rare resources. Ancient debris (the rare ore used to craft powerful Netherite gear) is hidden deep underground here. Nether quartz, soul sand, and nether wart provide materials for crafting, brewing, and building unique structures.

BIOMES

Nether Wastes, Soul Sand Valley, Basalt Deltas, Crimson Forest, Warped Forest

THE END BIOMES

The End is the final frontier - a strange, floating world of endless skies and eerie silence. The End barrens are quiet and empty, perfect for sneaking around before the big showdown. Obsidian pillars reach up to the skies in the highlands, home to the legendary ender dragon.

But there's more to the End than just the dragon - the rolling lands of the midlands are dotted with chorus plants and enderman, while the end islands scatter far and wide, hiding rare resources (like the elytra).

BIOMES

The End, End Barrens, End Highlands, End Midlands, Small End Islands

Looking for purpur blocks? End cities are literally made from them, and full of loot like emeralds and enchanted gear.

FIND STEVE AND ALEX

STEVE AND ALEX HEADED UNDERGROUND TO DO SOME MINING, BUT THOSE CAVES CAN GET SUPER CONFUSING! THINK YOU CAN FIND WHERE THEY ENDED UP? FLIP TO PAGES 62–63 FOR THE ANSWERS.

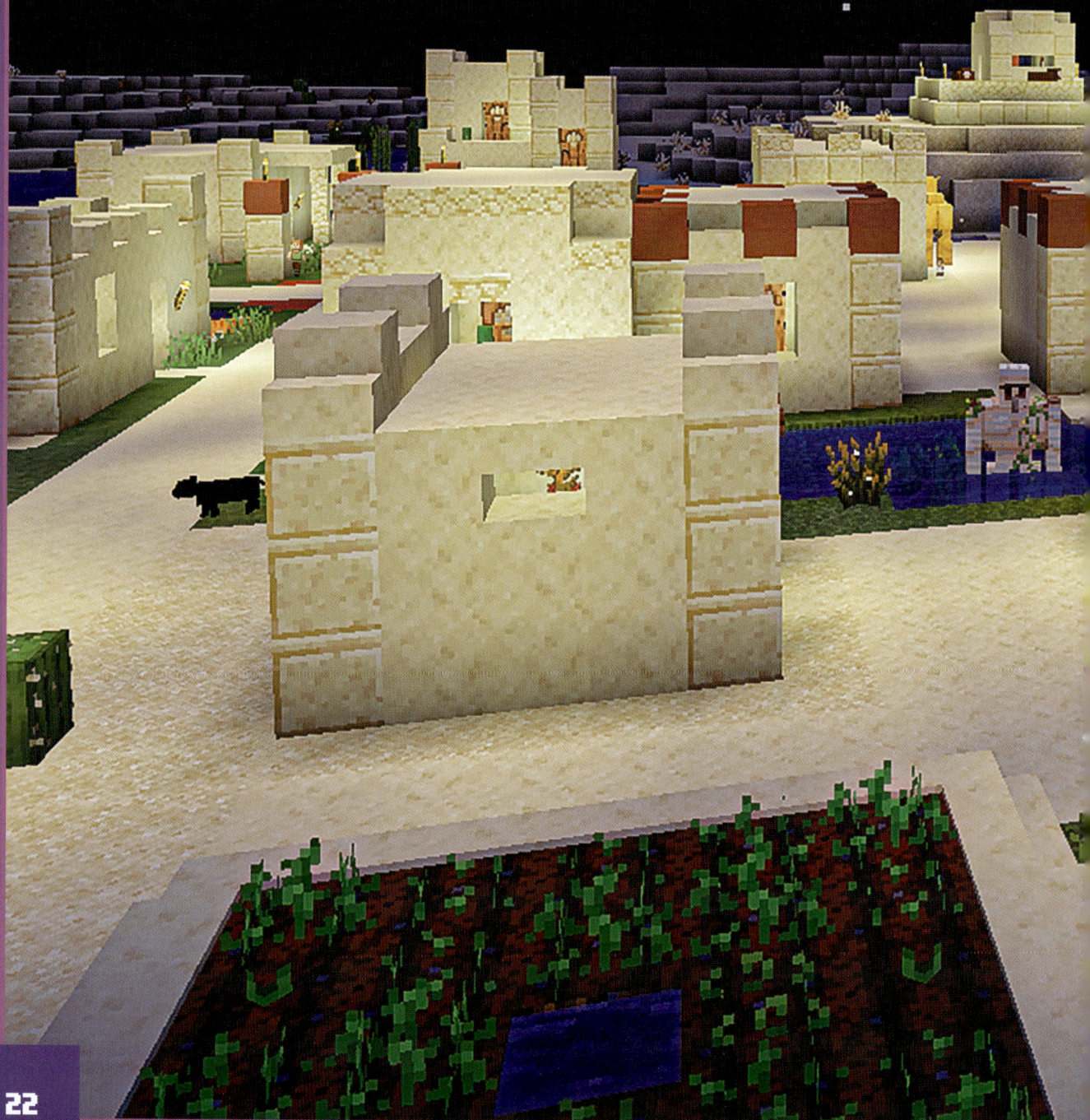

CHASE THE SKIES

THE SUMMER UPDATE 2025 CHASE THE SKIES BROUGHT A FRESH NEW BATCH OF SKYWARD ADVENTURES TO MINECRAFT. WITH A NEW MOUNT, STUNNING GRAPHICAL UPGRADES, AND GAMEPLAY IMPROVEMENTS, THIS UPDATE REFRESHED BOTH HOW THE GAME LOOKS AND HOW YOU PLAY IT. CHASE THE SKIES WAS ALL ABOUT ELEVATION - IN MORE WAYS THAN ONE.

TAKE TO THE SKIES

A new mob is automatically the highlight of any new update, and the Happy Ghast was no different. This inexplicably adorable giant blob brought a major new mode of transport to the game, letting players hop on and take to the skies instead of trekking around on foot or boat. The Happy Ghast took exploration to brand-new heights.

But a Happy Ghast isn't just something you'll stumble across in the wild: you'll need to put in a bit of love and care to get your very own.

- Find a dried ghast block in the Nether, either on the ground near Nether fossils in soul sand valleys. If you don't feel like searching around for one, you might get lucky and find a piglin who has one and is willing to barter.
- ...or, if you've already spent enough time in the Nether and have plenty of loot to show for it, you can also Craft one with soul sand and ghast tear x8.
- Revive your dried ghast by leaving it in water, where it'll eventually absorb enough to become a ghastling (stay hydrated, kids).
- Raise your ghastling and feed it snowballs to turn it into a Happy Ghast.

FIND YOUR FRIENDS

Can you even remember life before the Player Locator Bar? It replaced the old XP bar when teammates joined your world, and always kept an eye on your friends via colored dots and arrows, meaning you'll never lose them during explorations, tough fights, or solo trips out to refill the milk bucket (hey, they can get treacherous).

BECOME A BEAST MASTER

Leads took on a whole new leashing functionality, allowing you to leash multiple mobs together and create your very own line of loyal mobs to take on journeys with you. Saddles also became craftable, allowing you to create one on the go if you happen to stumble across a new mount on your travels.

BRILLIANT VISUALS

But the biggest quality of life update was the visual overhaul. This didn't affect gameplay directly, but it certainly had a huge effect on the game as a whole.

Vibrant Visuals is the game's first in-game shadow, improving lighting and bringing dynamic shadows, fog effects, reflective water and glowing ambient details (because the dead red eyes of spiders weren't quite creepy enough beforehand).

THE NEXT BIG UPDATE

WITH CHASE THE SKIES KEEPING THINGS EXCITING FOR NOW, IT MIGHT BE A LITTLE WHILE BEFORE THE NEXT MAJOR UPDATE SHAKES UP THE GAME. BUT WHY WAIT? IT'S YOUR TURN TO IMAGINE THE NEXT BIG THING! USE THE TEMPLATES TO DESIGN YOUR VERY OWN MINECRAFT UPDATE, FROM BLOCKS TO BIOMES AND BEYOND.

NEW BLOCKS FOR BUILDING

Let's start with the basics: new blocks! Think about what materials would make your update stand out. What's the vibe? What's the function? The possibilities are endless.

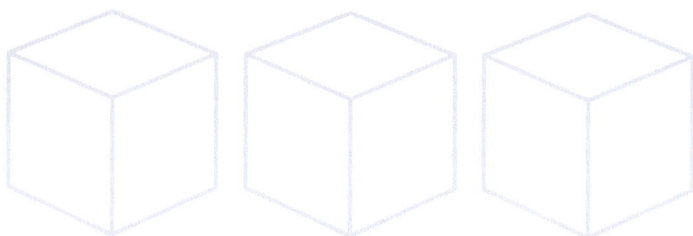

MEET NEW MOBS

Every major update brings new life to the world, and that means new mobs! What kind of creatures would you add? Are they friend or foe?

A NEW HOSTILE ENEMY

A NEW TYPE OF VILLAGER

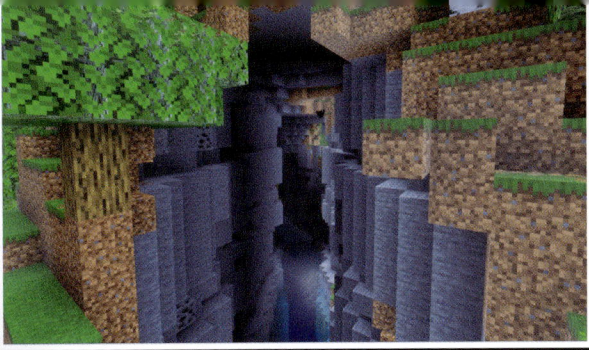

DISCOVER A NEW BIOME

The best updates always introduce new places to explore. What kind of biome would you create? Is it a frozen wasteland, a glowing jungle, or something totally out of this world?

BRAND NEW SKINS

Last but not least, you've got to look the part to explore your new world. Design some new skins that fit your update and bring your world to life with new characters to play as.

MINECRAFT MOBS

MOBS ARE WHAT MAKE MINECRAFT FEEL ALIVE, AND KEEP YOU ON YOUR TOES. SOME ARE CHILL AND JUST WANT TO HANG OUT, WHILE OTHERS ARE MORE INTO MAIMING AND MURDER. KNOWING YOUR MOBS MEANS THE DIFFERENCE BETWEEN A QUICK TRIP BACK TO BED AND COMING OUT ON TOP EVERY TIME.

PASSIVE MOBS

These mobs are more than happy to just share some space with you; some might even tag along on your expeditions. Passive mobs won't fight back, even if you provoke them.

Mob	Info
Allay	Can seek out items for you.
Axolotl	Can follow you into battle underwater.
Bat	N/A
Camel	Can be used as a mount (up to two players).
Cat	Can ward off phantoms and creepers.
Chicken	Drops feathers and raw chicken.
Cod	Drops raw cod and bonemeal.
Cow	Drops leather and raw beef.
Donkey	Can be used as a mount (with built-in inventory).
Fox	Bred foxes will defend you against mobs.
Frog	Drops froglights after eating magma cubes.

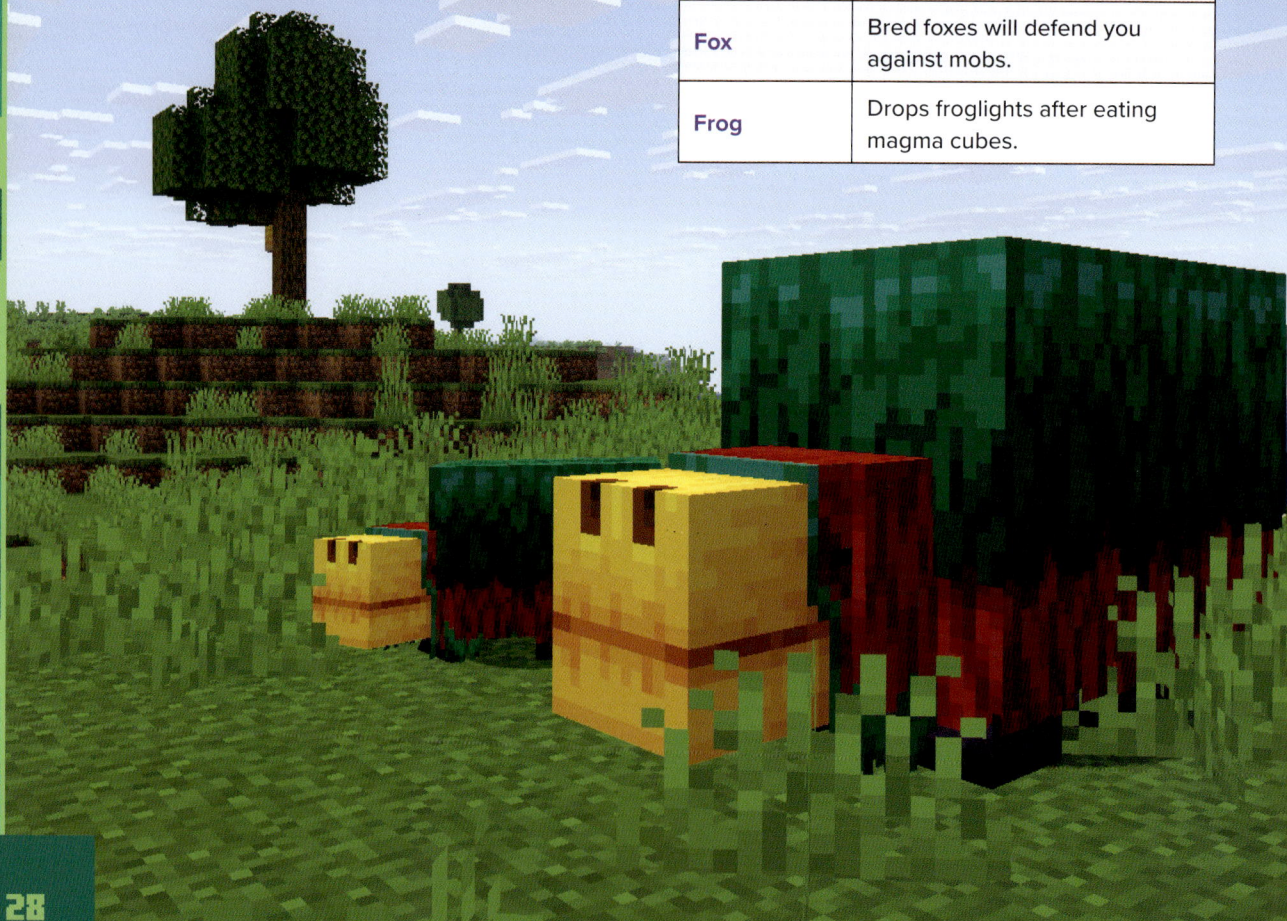

Mob	Info
Glow squid	Drops glow ink sacs.
Horse	Can be used as a mount (with inventory).
Happy ghast	Can be used as a flying mount.
Mooshroom	Drops leather and raw beef.
Mule	Can be used as a mount (with inventory).
Ocelot	Can ward off phantoms and creepers.
Snow golem	Can also be spawned by an enderman.
Parrot	Can detect hostile mobs within 20 blocks.
Pig	Drops pork chops.
Pufferfish	Drops bonemeal.
Rabbit	Drops rabbit hide, raw rabbit and rabbit's foot.
Salmon	Drops raw salmon.

Mob	Info
Sheep	Drops wool and mutton.
Skeleton horse	The fastest mount in game, and can be tamed if their rider is killed.
Squid	Drops ink sacs.
Strider	Drops string. Can be a mount in the Nether.
Tadpole	Grow into frogs.
Tropical fish	Drops tropical fish and bonemeal.
Turtle	Drops sea grass.
Villager	Useful for trading and other services.
Wandering trader	Drops milk bucket.
Villager	Useful for trading and other services.
Wandering trader	Drops milk bucket.

NEUTRAL MOBS

Neutral mobs have got their own thing going on and are happy to ignore you... unless you start causing a problem. Mess with them, and they won't hesitate to strike back.

Mob	Info
Bee	Can be farmed to collect honey and honeycomb.
Cave spider	Drops string and spider eyes.
Dolphin	Drops raw cod.
Drowned	Copper ingot, Trident
Enderman	Drops ender pearls.
Goat	Drops goat horns.
Iron golem	Killing a village Iron Golem lowers the player's village popularity by 10.
Llama	Can be used as a mount (with inventory).
Donkey	Can be used as a mount (with built-in inventory).
Fox	Bred foxes will defend you against mobs.
Frog	Drops froglights after eating magma cubes.
Panda	Drops bamboo.
Piglin	Drops whatever it is holding.
Polar bear	Drops raw cod and raw salmon.
Spider	Drops string and spider eyes.
Trader llama	Can be used as a mount (with built-in inventory).
Wolf	Can be tamed and helps the player in battle.
Zombified piglin	Drops gold nuggets and gold ingots.

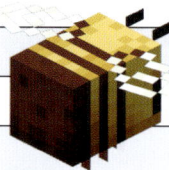

HOSTILE MOBS

Hostile mobs won't wait for you to aggravate - they stay aggro. They'll attack you the moment you stray into their detection zone (which can range from 16 to 100 blocks away).

Mob	Drop
Blaze	Blaze rod
Bogged	Bones, Arrows, Arrows of poison, Damaged bow
Breeze	Breeze rod
Chicken jockey	N/A
Creaking	N/A
Creeper	Gunpowder
Drowned	Copper ingot, Trident
Elder guardian	Prismarine shard, Wet sponge, Raw cod
Endermite	N/A
Evoker	Totem of undying, Emerald, Ominous banner
Ghast	Ghast tear, Gunpowder
Guardian	Raw cod, Prismarine crystal
Hoglin	Raw pork chop, Leather
Husk	Iron ingot
Magma cube	Magma cream
Phantom	Phantom membrane
Piglin brute	Golden axe
Pillager	Crossbow, Ominous banner
Ravager	Saddle
Shulker	Shulker shell
Silverfish	N/A
Skeleton	Bone, arrow
Skeleton horseman	N/A
Slime	Slimeball
Spider jockey	N/A
Stray	Bone, Arrow, Arrow of slowness
Vex	N/A
Vindicator	Emerald, Ominous banner, Iron axe
Warden	Sculk catalyst
Witch	Glass bottle, Glowstone dust, Gunpowder, Redstone, Spider eye, Sugar
Wither skeleton	Bone, Coal, Wither skeleton skull, Sword
Zoglin	N/A
Zombie	Iron ingot
Zombie villager	Iron ingot

BOSS MOBS

Boss mobs take hostility to the next level. Designed to challenge even the toughest players, they pack serious health, heavy damage, and zero patience - a deadly combination.

Boss	Drop
Ender Dragon	The Ender Dragon rules over the End dimension and stands as Minecraft's ultimate boss fight. With massive health and immunity to all status effects, she's a tough opponent. Defeat her, and you'll be rewarded with a dragon egg and a massive 12,000 XP.
Wither	Players can summon Withers to challenge themselves. When hurt, a Wither smashes all blocks in a 3x4x3 area around it, making it the only mob that can destroy Obsidian. Defeating it rewards you with a Nether Star and 50 XP.

KNOW YOUR BLOCKS

THE CORE OF EVERY MINECRAFT WORLD IS THE BLOCK: SIMPLE, HUMBLE, AND ABSOLUTELY ESSENTIAL. BLOCKS BUILD EVERYTHING ACROSS THE GAME'S THREE HUGE DIMENSIONS AND THEIR COUNTLESS UNIQUE ENVIRONMENTS.

THERE ARE... MAYBE... 200, OR SO, BLOCKS IN GAME, SO THIS HANDY GUIDE COVERS SOME OF THE MOST USEFUL AND COMMON BLOCKS YOU'RE LIKELY TO ENCOUNTER OR USE ON YOUR ADVENTURES.

NATURAL BLOCKS

These blocks naturally generate in the world and can be gathered to craft new items. You'll find natural blocks in both the Overworld and the Nether, and they mostly fall into five main groups.

Natural Blocks

GROUND	Info
Dirt	Farming's basic block, and an early building one too.
Mycelium	A dirt alternative found in mushroom island biomes.
Sand	Smelt sand to make glass, or mix with gunpowder to craft TNT.

PLANTS	Info
Cactus	Cactus blocks hurt anything they touch, and can only be grown in sand.
Grass	Till it with a hoe for an excellent farmland block.
Log	Logs can be crafted into planks and sticks to go on to make many other items.
Melon, Pumpkin etc.	Great food resources.

LIQUIDS	Info
Lava	This can be used to create stone and obsidian.
Water	An absolute must for farming, and always good to have on hand to deal with unexpected fires.

STONE	Info
Bedrock	The indestructible foundation block of the Overworld.
Gravel	Gravel (and sand) are affected by gravity, so they can collapse on a player (or mob) if broken above their head.
Obsidian	Obsidian is required for Nether portals, and can only be damaged by the wither boss.
Sandstone	A firmer form of sand that's great for building.

ORES AND MINERALS	Info
Coal Ore	A common ore useful for items like torches.
Copper Ore	Copper is the only block that changes its appearance over time. To prevent discoloration, be sure to wax copper with honeycomb.
Diamond Ore	A rare ore great for tools and armour.
Gold Ore	A rare ore that drops gold if mined with an iron pickaxe (at minimum).
Iron Ore	A common ore that is a makes a good pick for early pickaxes.
Lapis Lazuli Ore	A rare ore needed to fuel enchantment, make dyes and decorations.
Redstone Ore	An ore that drops redstone, a valuable resource for mechanical creations.

Different ores spawn at different coordinates, so here's the best depths to look for each:

Ore	Location	Note
Coal	Y=0 to Y=256	Optimal spawn point is around Y=90.
Copper	Y=-16 to Y=-112	Likely to be found in Dripstone Caves, around Y=48.
Diamond	Y=-64 to Y=16	The deeper you dig, the more likely this is to show up.
Emerald	Y=-16 to Y=236	More likely to spawn overground, at Y=224.
Gold	Y=-64 to Y-32	Generates in low quantities at Y=-16. Gold spawns more often in the Nether.
Iron	Y=-32 to Y=256	Very commonly found ore.
Lapis Lazuli	Y=-64 to Y=64	Very rare, but more likely to be found at Y=0.
Redstone	Y=-64 to Y=-32	The deeper you dig, the more likely this is to show up.

STRUCTURAL BLOCKS

You can find these blocks out in the world, usually as part of generated structures. They're perfect for collecting and using in your own builds.

Block	Info
Cobblestone	An excellent base construction material. Also comes in mossy and deepslate decorative variations.
Concrete	Created when concrete powder and water mix, it can also be found dyed in trial ruins.
Stone Brick	A block found in stronghold structures. Also comes in a mossy decorative variation.
Purpur	A purple block found in end cities and end ships.
Terracotta	A structural block found in badland biomes and deserts villages. Can be dyed and glazed.

NETHER BLOCKS

Some blocks only exist in the Nether. They're tougher to get your hands on, but totally worth it since they're among the best resources in the game.

Block	Info
Glowstone	Emits the highest level of light in the game.
Nether Brick	A very strong building material.
Netherrack	A great resource for bonfires.
Soul Sand	This block does a little bit of everything. It slows down movement, making it useful for defense, and it's also key for planting nether wart and summoning the wither.

DECORATIVE BLOCKS

Sometimes blocks are just here to serve looks. There are loads of decorative options that are perfect for adding style and personality to your home.

Block	Info
Froglight	Emits light and is made from a frog eating a magma cube.
Glass	Made by melting sand in a furnace, and can be tinted with dye.
Wool	Obtained from sheep and can be dyed.

SCULK BLOCKS

This eerie set of blocks only shows up in the Deep Dark biome. Most sculk blocks drop XP when broken - except for sculk vein, but let's be honest, no one's losing sleep over that one.

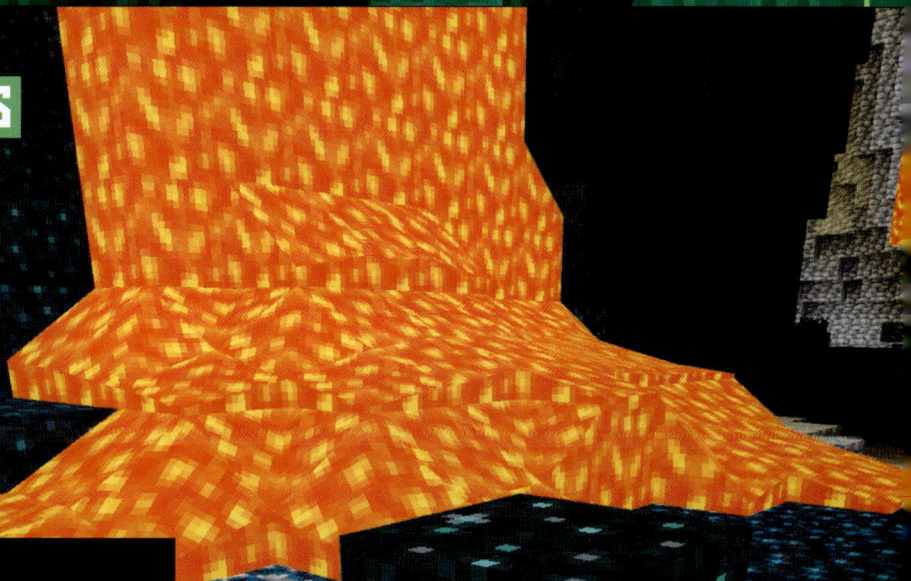

Block	Info
Sculk	Drops 1 XP.
Sculk Catalyst	Drops 5 XP. Converts surrounding blocks into sculk blocks.
Sculk Sensor	Drops 5 XP. Detects vibrations and triggers sculk shriekers.
Sculk Shrieker	Drops 5 XP. Summons a warden mob if triggered.

MINECRAFT MASTERCHEF

THE ULTIMATE COOKING KIT

Before you can whip up a feast in Minecraft, you'll need the right gear. No great chef enters a kitchen empty-handed, so if you're serious about crafting culinary greatness, this is your kit to go from survival mode to masterchef in no time.

Crafting Table:
The heart of every recipe (wooden plank x4)

Furnace:
Turn raw ingredients into delicious meals (cobblestone x8)

Fishing Rod:
Your ticket to fresh fish (stick x3, string x2)

Boat:
Set sail for some open-water fishing (wooden plank x5)

Bowl:
A humble must-have for soups and stews (wooden plank x3)

Bone Meal:
Max out your crop-growing game (bone x1)

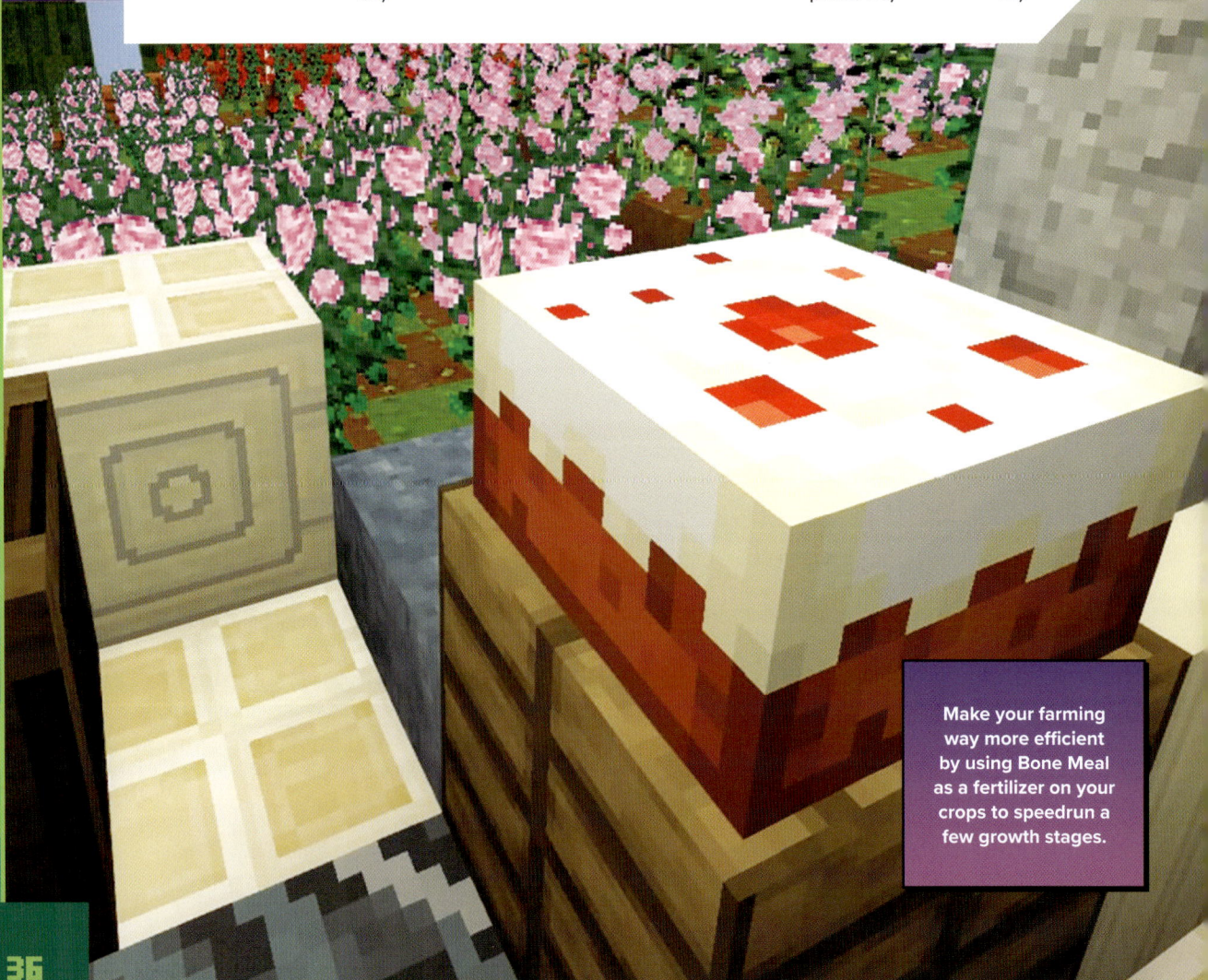

Make your farming way more efficient by using Bone Meal as a fertilizer on your crops to speedrun a few growth stages.

MINECRAFT MEATS

When it comes to restoring your hunger bar quickly and efficiently, meat is one of the best food sources in the game. Whether you're farming or hunting, cooked meat will keep you full and fighting-fit.

Meats are a great resource and one of the best (and most efficient) foods in the game to bring up your hunger bar.

Survival tip - if you're desperate and have no choice but to eat rotten flesh (we won't judge), drink a bucket of milk straight after. It'll cancel the poison effect and keep you going until you find something better.

Mob	Meat	Hunger Points (Raw)	Hunger Points (Cooked)
Cow	Beef	+3	+8
Mooshroom			
Pig	Pork	+3	+8
Chicken	Chicken	+2 (30% chance of food poisoning)	+6
Sheep	Mutton	+2	+6
Rabbit	Rabbit	+3	+5
Zombie	Rotten Flesh	+4 (80% chance of food poisoning)	N/A

FRESH FISH

That fishing rod and boat from your chef kit? It's time to put them to use. Drifting across the water while casting a line is more than just relaxing, it's one of the easiest ways to catch reliable food.

Fish	Hunger Points (Raw)	Hunger Points (Cooked)
Fish	+2	+5
Salmon	+2	+6
Clownfish	+2	N/A

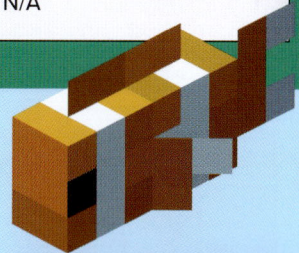

Did you know that fishing in rainy biomes can massively boost your chances of landing a catch (and we're talking both fish and treasure here).

FRUIT, VEG AND FARMING FINDS

Minecraft's world is bursting with edible plants just waiting to be harvested. From apples in trees to melons in jungles and carrots from village farms, there's no shortage of snacks. And the best part? Once you find them, you can replant and grow more.

Produce isn't just good for staying full; it's the gift that keeps on giving. Grab your seeds, find some soil, and start your own food empire one block at a time.

LEVEL UP YOUR MENU

In Minecraft, food isn't just fuel: it's an art form. Sure, keeping your hunger bar full is the goal, but why stop there? Sometimes, it's about turning the everyday into the extraordinary and bringing a little five-star flair to your furnace. They say that a well-fed adventurer can't be beat, right?

GOLDEN APPLE
Effects: Regeneration II, Absorption
Recipe: Gold Ingot x8, Apple x1

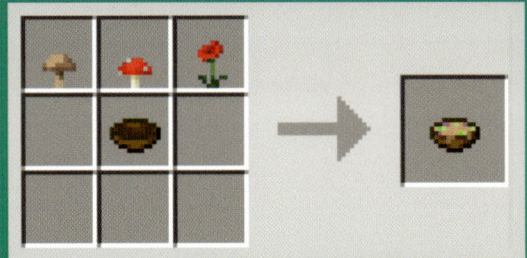

SUSPICIOUS STEW
Effects: Night Vision
Recipe: Brown Mushroom x1, Red Mushroom x1, Poppy x1, Bowl x1

SUSPICIOUS STEW
Effects: Fire Resistance
Recipe: Brown Mushroom x1, Red Mushroom x1, Allium x1, Bowl x1

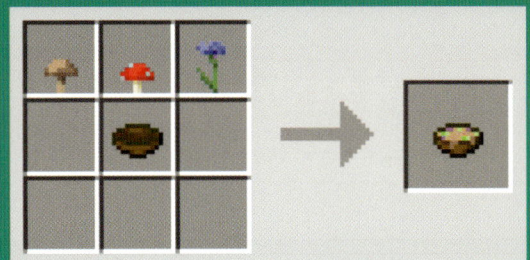

SUSPICIOUS STEW
Effects: Jump Boost
Recipe: Brown Mushroom x1, Red Mushroom x1, Cornflower x1, Bowl x1

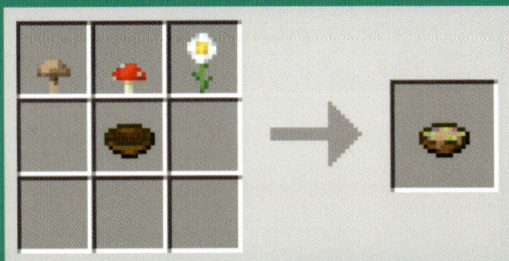

SUSPICIOUS STEW
Effects: Regeneration
Recipe: Brown Mushroom x1, Red Mushroom x1, Oxeye Daisy x1, Bowl x1

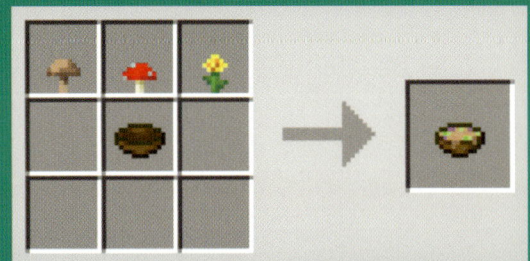

SUSPICIOUS STEW
Effects: Saturation
Recipe: Brown Mushroom x1, Red Mushroom x1, Dandelion x1, Bowl x1

BLOCKSEARCH

MINECRAFT IS RICH WITH BLOCKS AND RESOURCES - HIDING UNDERGROUND WITHIN THE DARKEST, DANKEST CAVES, DAZZLING UP HIGH IN THE SKIES AT THE TOPS OF MOUNTAINS OR GLOWING DEEP WITHIN THE DEPTHS OF THE NETHER. CAN YOU FIND THE DIFFERENT BLOCKS OF MINECRAFT IN THE WORDSEARCH BELOW? CHECK OUT P. 62-63 FOR ANSWERS.

N	C	J	H	B	H	F	D	L	D	C	B	G	D	Z	F	D
E	K	S	V	L	V	Y	Z	R	F	A	E	D	I	I	I	C
T	I	F	P	I	Y	E	I	H	M	Y	G	P	L	A	S	X
H	N	U	K	D	X	C	D	Q	Y	Z	R	U	M	O	L	H
E	T	E	M	I	R	O	R	G	A	I	Z	O	Y	X	G	B
R	Y	Q	T	V	P	P	U	A	S	A	N	N	M	W	X	S
Q	H	L	Y	H	X	P	N	M	L	D	S	O	P	X	N	W
U	B	E	Y	M	E	E	A	S	D	L	A	R	E	M	E	H
A	O	D	N	H	O	R	I	N	D	S	O	I	Q	H	S	V
R	R	V	G	R	I	P	I	E	N	O	T	S	D	E	R	R
T	W	R	P	N	A	L	Y	T	A	Q	U	H	M	D	T	G
Z	E	M	E	L	W	D	T	O	E	K	J	S	I	E	V	K
H	M	D	F	Q	S	H	G	P	R	Z	S	W	A	E	K	W
R	C	R	H	G	Y	E	T	K	Y	N	H	G	K	U	J	Z
B	L	Z	W	F	J	T	A	J	O	N	H	T	Z	Q	S	Y
I	I	G	Y	X	K	G	G	N	N	D	K	S	P	V	F	Q
G	L	O	W	S	T	O	N	E	Y	M	S	T	B	P	T	N

Copper
Diamond
Emerald
Gold

Iron
Lapis Lazuli
Glowstone

Netherite
Nether Quartz
Prismarine
Redstone

HOME SWEET HOME

EVERY ADVENTURER NEEDS A BASE CAMP, NOT JUST FOR STASHING LOOT, BUT FOR KICKING OFF THOSE ENCHANTED BOOTS AND TAKING A BREATHER. I KNOW BUILDING A HOME IS PROBABLY THE LAST THING ON YOUR MIND WHEN IT COMES TO EXPLORING THE HIDDEN WOODLAND MANSION YOU SPOTTED IN THE WOODS OR A SUPER INVITING GAPING MAW IN THE BASE OF A MOUNTAIN. WHY BUILD A HOME WHEN I COULD BE OUT THERE EXPLORING?

BECAUSE EVEN THE MOST HARDCORE OF ADVENTURERS NEED SOMEWHERE SAFE TO CRASH. MINECRAFT ISN'T JUST A GAME OF EXPLORATION; IT'S A GAME OF SURVIVAL, AND REST, UNFORTUNATELY, IS A MAJOR PART OF ENSURING THE LATTER. A HOME LETS YOU HEAL, PROTECTS YOU FROM CREEPERS, AND SERVES AS A PLACE TO STASH YOUR HARD-EARNED TREASURES. IT'S NOT JUST A HOUSE - IT'S YOUR HEADQUARTERS.

It can be a little intimidating just staring at an empty plot of land with all the possibilities in the world out there. Try checking out some of the free maps on the Minecraft Marketplace for inspiration - you'll see what structural wonders you can build with blocks!

WHERE SHOULD I SETTLE DOWN?

There's no single "best" spot to build a base, it all depends on your vibe. Some players love the peaceful hum of flower fields, others are all about oceanside views or dramatic snowy cliffs. But regardless of your aesthetic, here are a few things to look out for:

- Nearby resources like wood, food, and ore.
- Easy access to water (perfect for building a dock for fishing and being able to sail out on your boat).
- A bit of elevation for better mob defense.
- Plenty of space to bring your house vision to life.

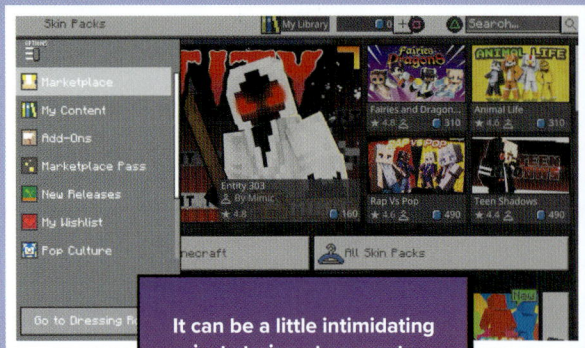

SO HOW DO I BUILD A HOME?

Totally up to you - that's the magic of Minecraft. But if you want a solid starting point, here's a basic step-by-step:

1. PUT UP SOME WALLS
Start simple: four walls, leave space for doors and windows. Use non-flammable materials like stone (you don't want your house catching fire the first time lightning strikes).

2. SECURE THE ENTRY POINTS
Gaps are fine for airflow, but they also let skeletons snipe you in your sleep (not ideal). Craft some doors and glass to keep things cosy and safe.

3. GO BIG (OR UNDERGROUND)
Once you've got the basics, start customizing! Add a second floor, dig a basement, build a rooftop garden-whatever you want.

4. LIGHT IT UP
Darkness = danger. Place torches (or spring for a fancier option like glowstone or froglights) to keep mobs away and also set the mood.

5. ADD THE ESSENTIALS
First priority should be a bed so that you can set your spawn point. After that, think chests, crafting tables, furnaces, maybe a tiny crop patch for food. Boom: functional and fabulous.

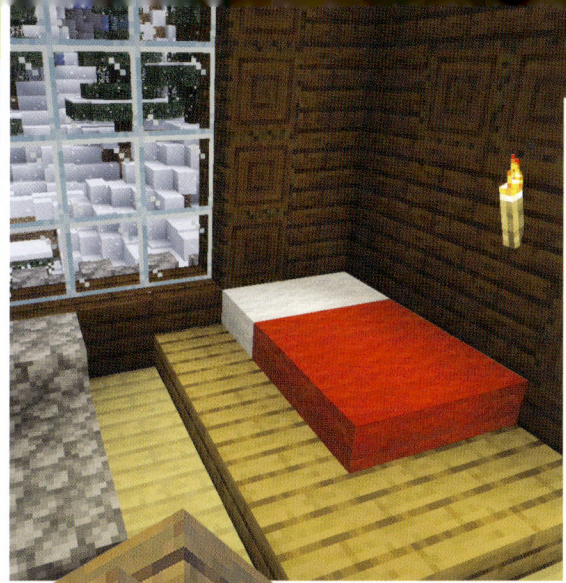

Want some company at your home while also making it safer? Tame a cat or ocelot with some raw fish to get your very own feline housemate. Not only are they cute, but they also keep creepers at bay (that's how they pay the rent).

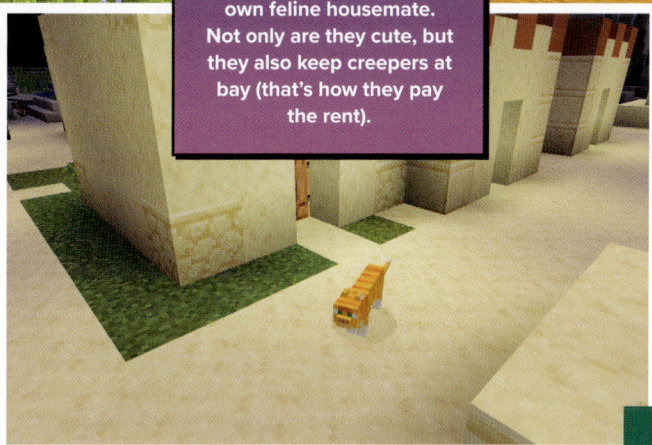

Feeling a little lazy or just want roommates? Why not an empty house in a village? Or... just snap an occupied one if you prefer its vibe. The villagers might not love it... but hey, they'll get over it.

ADVENTURER'S CROSSWORD

MINECRAFT HAS A WHOLE PLETHORA OF MAGICAL PLACES TO EXPLORE, BUT EVERY ADVENTURER WORTH THEIR SALT KNOWS HOW TO IDENTIFY THE GAME'S STRUCTURES - WHETHER THEY'RE STUMBLED UPON BY ACCIDENT OR DELIBERATELY SOUGHT OUT TO FIND A RARE TREASURE. PROVE YOUR ADVENTURING PROWESS BY SOLVING THE CLUES AND FILLING OUT THE CROSSWORD WITH THE GAME'S DIFFERENT EXPLORABLE STRUCTURES. CHECK OUT P. 62-63 FOR ANSWERS.

ACROSS

2. This underwater structure is home to the Drowned. (5, 5)
5. Wither skeletons and blazes call this structure home. (6, 8)
6. This haunting structure is home to the legendary elytra. (3, 4)
9. This underground chamber consists of copper and tuff blocks. (5, 7)
10. This maze of corridors can be found in the badlands, and are covered in cobwebs. (9)

DOWN

1. These massive prismarine temples house guardians. (8)
3. Found in the deep dark, this structure has long corridors made of deepslate and wool. (7, 4)
4. Seek out this structure to find an end portal. (10)
7. These small wooden buildings are sometimes occupied by witches. (5, 3)
8. This explorable vessel once sailed the sea's surface. (9)

FRIENDLY MOBSEARCH

NOT EVERYTHING IN THE MINECRAFT WORLD IS OUT FOR YOUR PIXELATED BLOOD; THERE ARE PLENTY OF FRIENDLY MOBS OUT THERE TOO! CAN YOU FIND THE FRIENDLY MOBS IN THE MOBSEARCH BELOW? CHECK OUT P. 62-63 FOR ANSWERS.

T	O	C	Y	H	K	D	E	Z	D	X	O	C	M	Y	I	N
I	F	Z	A	E	S	S	N	P	W	L	B	H	G	U	S	G
B	S	L	B	M	R	I	A	M	L	T	F	I	Q	O	L	K
B	M	B	R	O	E	R	F	I	X	T	C	C	J	X	N	E
A	W	Q	H	E	R	L	D	R	N	O	B	K	F	D	W	F
R	C	D	S	O	G	A	C	O	E	W	F	E	H	Q	J	N
V	Y	I	T	H	M	A	M	C	W	F	C	N	Q	F	G	Q
A	X	U	X	R	C	L	L	E	S	R	F	S	H	E	E	P
O	H	Q	A	Q	A	N	A	L	Z	W	T	U	R	Q	D	Z
K	V	S	K	S	S	B	C	O	I	A	Y	Y	Y	P	O	S	Y
L	U	W	T	R	H	S	I	T	D	V	V	Q	N	Z	T	A
A	X	O	L	O	T	L	N	P	E	W	L	K	I	X	R	L
A	P	L	G	I	P	F	O	I	D	V	E	Y	V	T	I	L
D	N	G	F	X	T	L	V	M	F	Y	G	O	R	F	D	A
X	S	J	B	I	E	L	F	U	R	F	D	G	D	U	E	N
M	O	O	S	H	R	O	O	M	F	H	E	Q	J	Q	R	K
E	L	T	R	U	T	U	U	B	H	D	J	R	P	A	U	W

Allay	Frog	Ocelot	Sheep
Armadillo	Fox	Parrot	Sniffer
Axolotl	Glow Squid	Pig	Strider
Camel	Horse	Pufferfish	Tadpole
Chicken	Mooshroom	Rabbit	Turtle
Donkey	Mule	Salmon	Villager

43

PRO-SURVIVAL TIPS

YOU'VE MADE IT PAST THE WOODEN TOOLS AND DIRT HUTS STAGE. YOU'VE GOT A DECENT HOUSE, A STACK OF IRON, AND YOU KNOW HOW TO SWING A SWORD. COOL. NOW IT'S TIME TO SHIFT GEARS FROM "SURVIVOR" TO "UNSTOPPABLE." THESE ARE THE TIPS SEASONED PLAYERS USE TO STAY AHEAD OF THE CURVE - AND ALIVE.

GET ENCHANTING ASAP

The enchantment table is not strictly end-game - it's an early game power-up if you're willing to put the work in.

Step one is crafting an enchanting table. You'll need four obsidian blocks, two diamonds, and a book to make it happen. Once it's set up, you'll power your enchantments using a mix of lapis lazuli and experience levels - the more you've got, the better your options. There are around thirty different types of enchantment to choose from and different rankings within each type, but even low-level enchantments like Protection I or Efficiency I give a massive boost to your gameplay.

FIGHT SMART

Minecraft's combat rewards precision. If you're still charging in with full swings, then you're leaving battle wins on the table. Try to time your attacks for critical hits by aiming from midair for max damage. Use your shield to stagger mobs like skeletons and pillagers, then punish their cooldown.

Also consider your battlefield as part of your strategy. Great warriors use the terrain to their advantage - water can stall mobs and break line of sight, high ground gives you advantage and reach, and block placement in real time can stop enemies dead in their tracks.

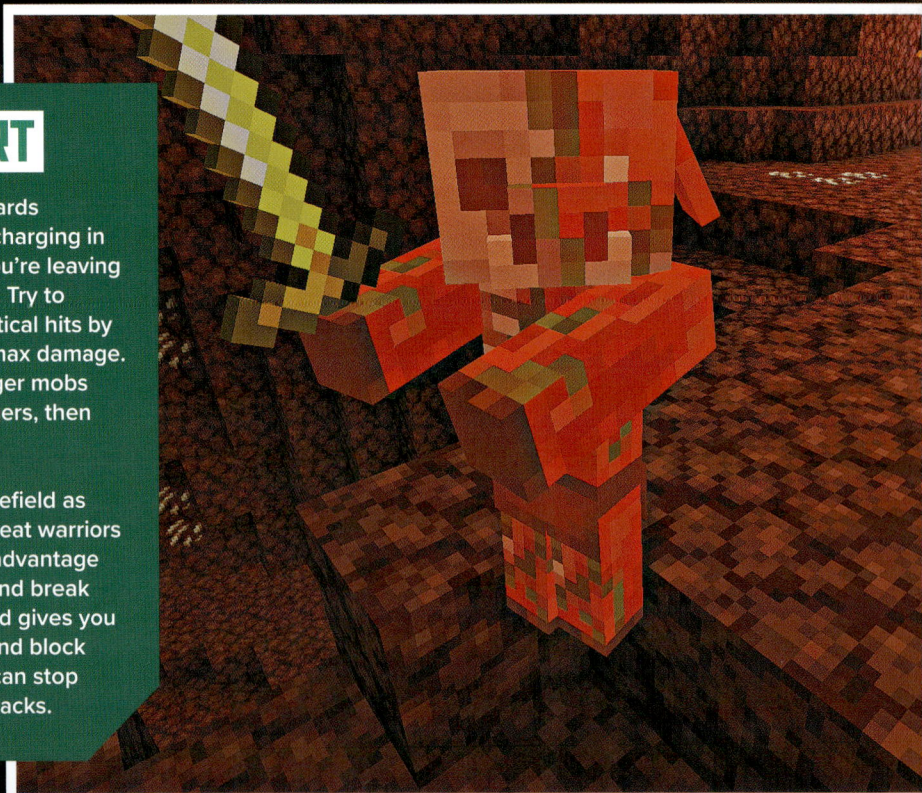

MINE SMART

Mining isn't just digging a hole and hoping for diamonds - it's an art form. Never dig straight down unless you're trying to speedrun your way into a toasty lava bath; always dig diagonally. And when you head underground, be sure to bring the essentials: extra pickaxes, stacks of torches, food to keep you going, and a water bucket for lava panic moments.

Oh, and don't ignore the standard ores. Iron, coal, and copper might not sparkle, but they're clutch early-game. Skip them now, and you'll be kicking yourself later.

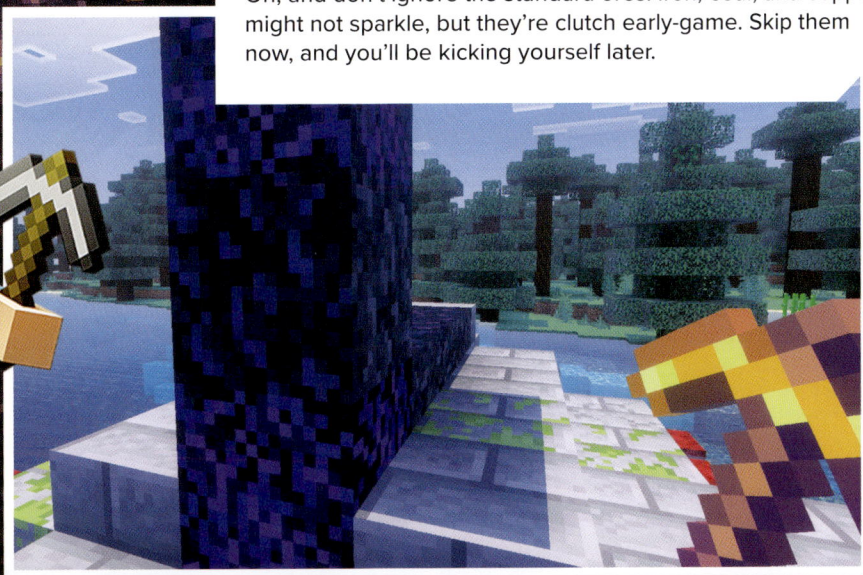

INVENTORY MANAGEMENT

You might think your sharpest weapon is that enchanted diamond sword or the trusty pickaxe that's carried you through five biomes and a boss fight. But the real MVP of survival? It's your inventory.

Minecraft is a game of resources, and your survival hinges on how well you manage them. When things go sideways (or downwards, if you suddenly find yourself plummeting through a cave ceiling), the difference between surviving and rage-quitting comes down to what's in your hotbar.

You've got 27 inventory slots to work with. The trick is balance. A pro loadout keeps your inventory lean, versatile, and mission-ready. It's best to split your 27 slots down into these categories: 2 weapons, 2 tools, 1 lighting, 1 food, 4 crafting utilities, 6 utility items, 4 potions, and 6 dealer's choice.

AND LASTLY... BUCKETS ARE S-TIER

Buckets are wildly underrated.

Water bucket: lifesaver from lava or fall damage.

Lava bucket: portable smelting fuel or emergency weapon.

Milk bucket: cures poison (thanks, cave spiders).

Carry one whenever you can, they're basically survival Swiss army knives.

MASTER YOUR CRAFT

CRAFTING IS KEY TO THE MINECRAFT EXPERIENCE; IT'S 50% OF THE GAME'S NAME. SURE, YOU CAN CREATE YOUR OWN ADVENTURE AND DO WHATEVER YOU PLEASE, BUT YOU'RE GOING TO NEED TO MAKE A LOT OF THINGS ON THE WAY - AND THAT'S WHERE THE TRUSTY OLD CRAFTING TABLE COMES INTO PLAY.

Sure, crafting tables excel at crafting (shocking revelation, we know), but they're also your go-to repair stop for battered tools, dented armor, and well-worn weapons.

CRAFTING GRID

Your inventory comes with a basic 2x2 grid that's perfect for quick, simple recipes on the move. Cute. But when you need to get serious (which you very much will, and very soon), you'll want that sweet 3x3 grid that only a crafting table can provide.

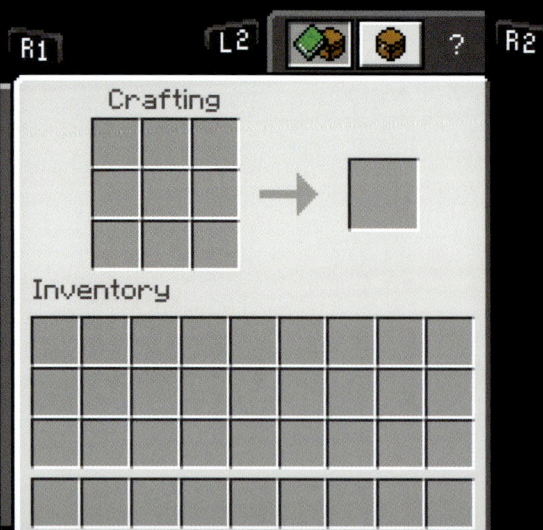

R1   L2   ?   R2

Crafting

→

Inventory

RECIPES

Your Recipe Book is basically your culinary bible, housing every crafting, smelting, and brewing recipe known to block-kind. New recipes unlock naturally as you explore - discover a new resource, set foot in an uncharted biome, or simply stumble upon the right combination of circumstances.

But hey, sometimes you're in a rush and you don't have time to fill out the recipe book via discovery. Sometimes you need to know how to make a birthday cake right this very moment (we won't ask questions). If so, then be sure to check out online crafting databases to find out how to make something specific.

New Recipe(s) Unlocked!
Check your recipe book

CRAFTING QUIZ

HOW WELL DO YOU KNOW YOUR CRAFT, ADVENTURER? SURE, YOU'RE NOT EXPECTED TO KNOW HOW TO MAKE GLAZED TERRACOTTA BY HEART - BUT THERE ARE RECIPES FOR MUST-HAVE KEY ITEMS THAT EVERY GREAT ADVENTURER HAS MEMORISED. TRY TO IDENTIFY THESE KEY INGREDIENT COMBOS BELOW, THEN CHECK OUT P. 62-63 TO SEE IF YOU KNOW YOUR RECIPES.

1

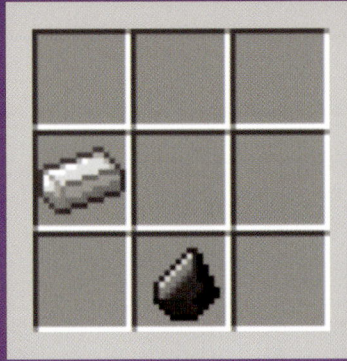

2

3

4

5

6

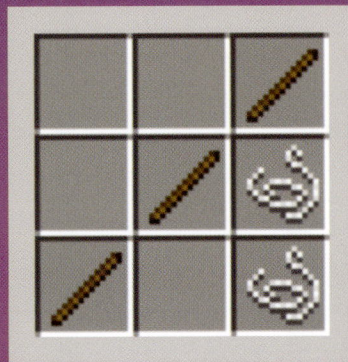

7

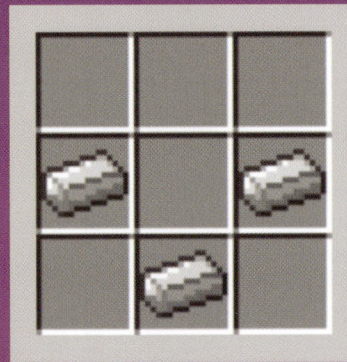

8

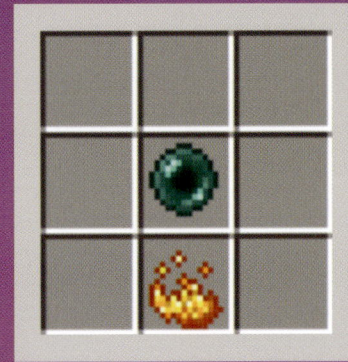

9

MINECRAFT MVPs

WHAT HAPPENS WHEN YOU GIVE CREATIVE MINDS INFINITE BLOCKS AND A RECORDING SETUP? YOU GET THE INDISPUTABLE KINGS AND QUEENS OF MINECRAFT - TITAN CREATORS COMMANDING AUDIENCES BIGGER THAN SOME LITERAL COUNTRIES (YOU'VE BEEN BEAT, NEPAL). LOOKING FOR EPIC ADVENTURES, HILARIOUS CHAOS, OR MIND-BLOWING BUILDS? THESE LEGENDS HAVE MASTERED EVERY CORNER OF MINECRAFT - AND THEY'RE DEFINITELY WORTH CHECKING OUT.

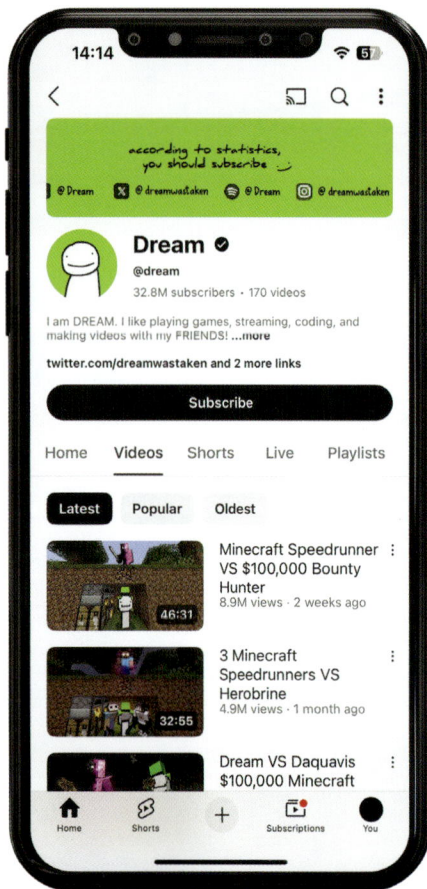

DanTDM

SUBSCRIBERS: 29+ MILLION
KNOWN FOR: MOD SHOWCASES

This British creator has been the friendly face of Minecraft since 2012, known for his mod showcases and genuine enthusiasm for everything the game has to offer. Dan makes every viewer feel welcome, like hanging out with your best block-centric friend. He's explored thousands of mods and created ongoing storylines that have kept fans engaged for over a decade.

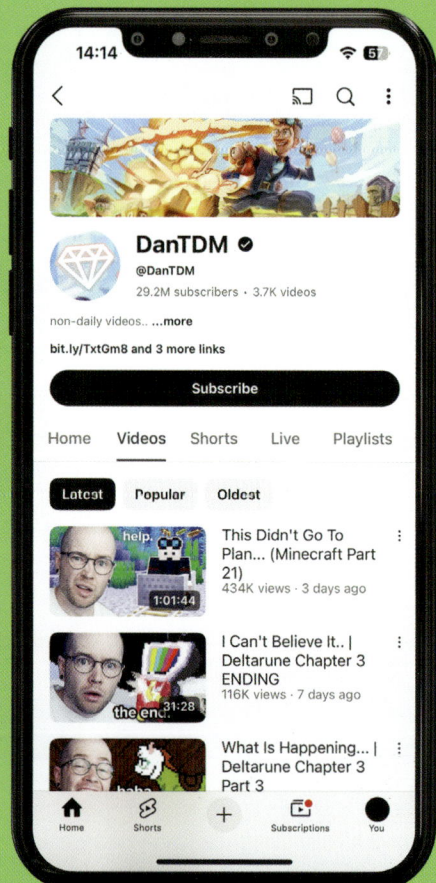

DREAM

SUBSCRIBERS: 31+ MILLION
KNOWN FOR: IMPOSSIBLE ESCAPES AND CLUTCH PLAYS

With over 31 million subscribers, Dream became famous for his incredible Minecraft Manhunt series, where he tries to beat the game while his friends hunt him down. His speedrunning skills and ability to think under pressure are legendary, and his videos regularly hit 100+ million views. Though he stepped back from regular content, his impact on competitive Minecraft is undeniable.

APHMAU

SUBSCRIBERS: 23+ MILLION
KNOWN FOR: EPIC ROLEPLAY STORIES

Aphmau has transformed Minecraft into a storytelling platform like no other creator. Her hit series like MyStreet and Minecraft Diaries feel more like watching TV shows than gaming content - with incredible voice acting and character development, she's proven that Minecraft can be a legitimate medium for compelling narratives about love, friendship, and adventure.

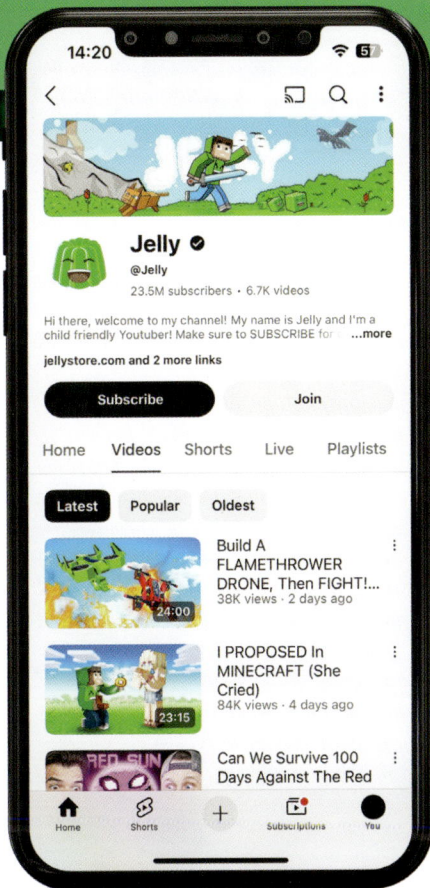

JELLY

SUBSCRIBERS: 23+ MILLION
KNOWN FOR: FAILURES AND CHAOS

This Dutch creator turns everything into comedy gold. Whether he's failing spectacularly at building a simple house or getting completely lost in his own base, Jelly somehow makes disaster look like the most fun you could possibly have. His videos with friends often descend into complete chaos, and that's exactly what makes them so addictive to watch.

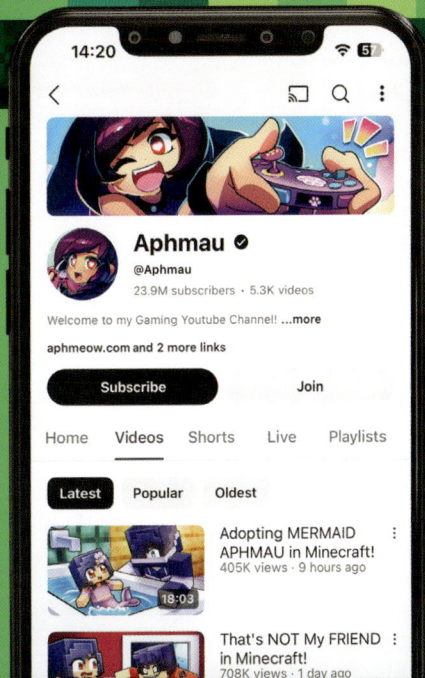

CAPTAINSPARKLEZ

SUBSCRIBERS: 11+ MILLION
KNOWN FOR: PARODY BOPS

One of the OG Minecraft legends, CaptainSparklez has been creating content since 2010. His parody songs are viral sensations (find me a hardcore Minecrafter who doesn't know Revenge by heart, I dare you), and his adventure map playthroughs have entertained millions since the game's earliest days.

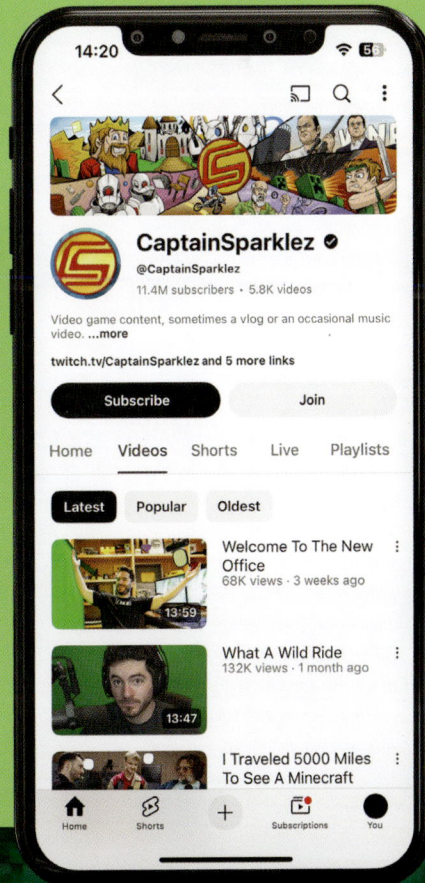

SPOT THE DIFFERENCE I

CAN YOU SPOT ALL EIGHT DIFFERENCES BETWEEN THESE TWO PICTURES? FLIP TO PAGES 62-63 TO CHECK YOUR ANSWERS!

DEEP DARK RUNNER

CAN YOU MAKE IT OUT OF THE DEEP DARK WITHOUT BUMPING INTO ANY OF THE SCULK SHRIEKERS, OR WORSE... THE WARDEN? CHECK OUT P. 62-63 FOR ANSWERS!

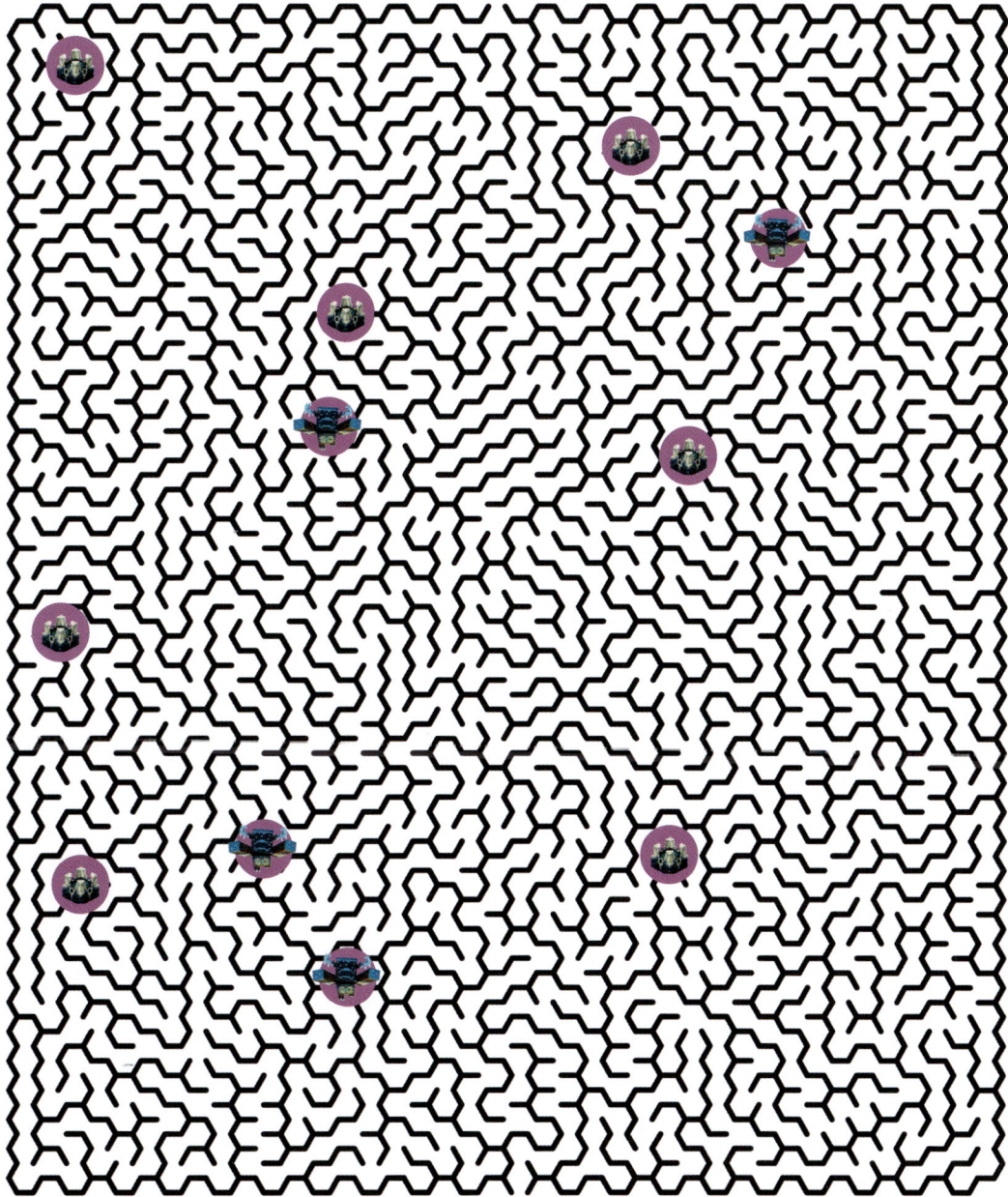

COMBAT 101

MINECRAFT ISN'T JUST ABOUT BUILDING CASTLES AND TAMING AXOLOTLS (THOUGH THEY ARE GREAT) - IT'S ALSO ABOUT SURVIVING THE NIGHT. WHETHER YOU'RE DEFENDING YOUR BASE FROM A ZOMBIE HORDE OR BRAVING THE NETHER, COMBAT IS A SKILL EVERY PLAYER NEEDS TO MASTER.

KNOW YOUR ENEMIES

Each mob in Minecraft has its own style of attack. Understanding how they behave is the first step toward beating them.

- **Creepers:** They don't make a sound until it's too late. Keep your distance, strike fast, and back away. Water helps reduce their explosion damage.
- **Zombies:** Slow but persistent, zombies group up real fast and can call in reinforcements. Use knockback to keep them at bay.
- **Skeletons:** These mobs are archers and pretty accurate from afar. Block incoming arrows with a shield and try to close the gap ASAP to stop them firing.
- **Spiders:** They can climb walls and leap at you. Watch for sudden jumps and try to lure them into open spaces to take away their advantage.
- **Endermen:** Leave them alone unless you're ready. If you do look at one, fight under a two-block-high ceiling to avoid their reach.
- **Witches:** These mobs use potions to heal and poison you. Hit hard and fast before they can react.

Heads up! Your ears can be just as important as your sword. Tweak your audio settings so you're not missing any subtle cues, especially footsteps. In Minecraft, player and mob footsteps are separate sound categories, so if you lower your own footstep volume, you'll be way more likely to catch something sneaking up behind you.

DIVERSIFY YOUR ARSENAL

The right tools can turn a risky fight into a breeze. You don't want to be bringing a pickaxe into a trident fight, so know which weapon gets what job done.

- **Swords:** Fast and reliable. Great for general melee combat.
- **Axes:** Deal more damage than swords but swing slower.
- **Bows:** Perfect for taking down mobs from a distance. Aim for a headshot for extra damage.
- **Crossbows:** Slower reload but more perful than bows. Use fireworks for explosive shots.
- **Tridents:** Rare but versatile. Can be thrown or used in melee. Enchant with Loyalty to make them return or Riptide to zoom through water.

You don't always need an enchanting table to score powerful gear. Every now and then, you might stumble across pre-enchanted items out in the wild. Keep an eye out for rare mob drops, raid an End City for high-tier loot, or try your luck trading with piglins or villagers. You never know when the game might throw you a magical freebie.

ENCHANTMENTS FOR A HELPING HAND

Enchantments are the best for giving you the edge in a tough situation. Not all Enchantments are made equal, and it's a lengthy process to experiment with, so here are some of the best enchantments for general combat:

- **Mending (I):** Wear and tear can take down even the highest-end gear, so this enchantment is always a good idea to protect your costly pieces. Mending gives XP bubbles the ability to repair, so you can repair your weapons after using them.
- **Sharpness (I-V):** While some enchantments only work with specific weapons (like Channeling for tridents or Piercing for crossbows) Sharpness is a solid all-rounder that increases damage across most melee weapons.
- **Power (I-V):** This enchantment gives a reliable boost to your bow's damage, making it another great pick to boost the strength of your ranged combat.
- **Protection (I-IV):** It's best to start with broad enchantments before diving into the more specialized ones. Protection reduces damage from a wide variety of sources, making it a strong first choice for any armor setup.

GUESS THE MOB

THINK YOU'VE GOT SHARP MOB-SPOTTING SKILLS? USE THE BEHAVIOUR CLUES BELOW TO FIGURE OUT WHICH MOB IS LURKING NEARBY. PUT YOUR MOB KNOWLEDGE TO THE TEST - THEN CHECK OUT P. 62-63 TO SEE HOW YOU DID!

1. **I can be saddled and ridden by two players.**

2. **I won't attack, but my defensive stance can inflict Poison.**

3. **Find me and my cub in cold biomes.**

4. **I can't move or attack if you're looking at me.**

5. **I won't be distracted with gold like the other Piglins.**

6. **I am blind and rely on my other senses to find my prey.**

7. **Defeat me if you need a blaze rod.**

8. **Stealing my trident is the only way you can get one.**

9. **Saddle me up and ride me over lava.**

10. **I'll collect and deliver whatever you need.**

COMMAND CENTER

MINECRAFT IS ONE OF THE MOST FUN GAMES TO MAKE YOUR OWN, AND COMMANDS ARE WHERE THE REAL MAGIC HAPPENS.

IF YOU'RE PLAYING ON A COMPUTER, THEN THE WORLD TRULY IS AT YOUR FINGERTIPS. WITH JUST A FEW KEYSTROKES, YOU CAN CALL IN SNIFFERS, ZIP ACROSS BIOMES, OR SOAR THROUGH THE SKIES LIKE YOU OWN THEM. WANT TO TRY IT OUT? THESE ARE SOME OF THE COOLEST AND MOST USEFUL COMMANDS TO GET YOU STARTED.

Command	Description
/teleport [target] <destination>	Zip yourself (or anyone else) straight to a set of coordinates with this handy teleport trick.
/weather <clear/rain/ thunder>	Not feeling the rain? Change up your current location's weather.
/time set <time>	Set the time of day, either using numbers (ex. "1000" for 10am) or expressions (ex. noon, night etc.).
/summon <entity> [x] [y] [z]	Tired of hoping for that ultra-rare spawn? Skip the wait and summon exactly what you want, right where you want it.
/kill [target]	Get ready to say goodbye because this command makes it quick.
/locate <category> <thing>	Don't feel like hunting down a biome or structure? Use this to find the nearest one's coordinates - then use the Teleport command straight there.
/gamemode <mode>	Want to jump between game modes (like trying to survive in your recently complete Creative build)? This command lets you switch it up instantly, no fuss.
/difficulty <difficulty>	Switch up your game's challenge level with this command without needing to reset.
/give <target> <item> <quantity>	Any in-game item can be yours (and in any quantity).
/enchant <target> <enchantment> [level]	Enchanting can be a grind, so don't feel bad about speeding things up with a couple of commands. Your secret's safe with us!

SPOT THE DIFFERENCE II

CAN YOU SPOT ALL EIGHT DIFFERENCES BETWEEN THESE TWO PICTURES? FLIP TO PAGES 62-63 TO CHECK YOUR ANSWERS!

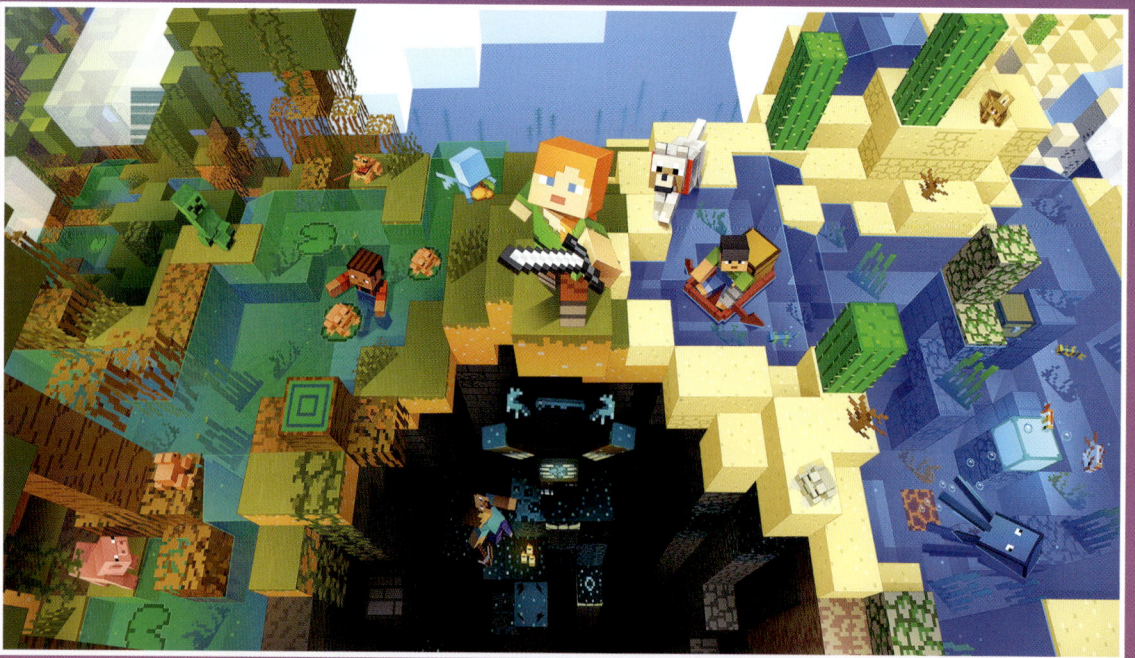

BLOCK SCRAMBLE

HOW WELL DO YOU KNOW YOUR BLOCKS? UNSCRAMBLE THESE CLUES AND TO FIND THE NAMES OF NINE MINECRAFT BLOCKS. CHECK OUT P. 62-63 FOR ANSWERS!

1. **GNEOPS**

2. **SNMPIRAERI**

3. **ECNCEOTR**

4. **REEDNSOT**

5. **COSHUR FUITR**

6. **URPPRU**

7. **TSALBA**

8. **BALNESCOTK**

9. **RNHTEE QTZAUR**

10. **OSLU DNAS**

MINECRAFT
THE MOVIE

2025 SAW MINECRAFT BREAK OUT BEYOND OUR COMPUTERS AND GAME CONSOLES, AND FINALLY MAKE ITS WAY ONTO THE BIG SCREEN. MINECRAFT: THE MOVIE TURNED A SANDBOX WORLD INTO A CINEMATIC ADVENTURE, DEFYING INITIAL RESERVATIONS (DON'T WORRY, THIS IS A SAFE SPACE - WE CAN ALL ADMIT THAT THE FIRST LOOK WAS A ROUGH TIME FOR US), BREAKING RECORDS AND TOTALLY REDEFINING WHAT A VIDEO GAME MOVIE COULD BE.

Sound familiar? The movie's soundtrack featured game tracks like C418's *Calm 1* playing in the Overworld, and Lena Raine's *Pigstep*.

THE JOURNEY TO THE BIG SCREEN

It may have been a given that Minecraft was big enough for its own movie, but the road to the big screen took time - over a decade, to put a number to it. After years of announcements followed by silence and stars joining and leaving, production finally kicked off in New Zealand in 2024 and wrapped within months.

The movie team wanted their film to be as true to the game as possible, so they decided that everything in the movie world had to work with Minecraft in-game physics: if it can't be built in Survival Mode, then it didn't make the cut. And that's exactly what happened to a scene with a massive Piglin trojan horse, which was left on the cutting room floor to stay faithful to in-game build mechanics. Another huge challenge was emulating the game's trademark, simplistic and pixelated style IRL. That task fell to Weta FX and Sony Imageworks, with Digital Domain coming in to add some finishing touches. These artists studied in-game lighting, particle physics and even block placement speed to ensure the movie matched the game's style, frame by frame.

BOX OFFICE SMASH

The movie may have taken some time to develop, but it certainly didn't take long to make an impression. Minecraft: The Movie exploded like a well-placed creeper. On opening weekend, it made over $300 million (USD), and by the end of the summer, it hit just below $1 billion (yeah, billion - with a b), making it the highest-grossing video game movie of all time.

Start Again

MINECRAFT ROYALTY

Sure, Jack Black and Jason Momoa headline, but did you recognise Minecraft royalty in the movie?

Minecraft YouTubers Mumbo Jumbo (Oliver Brotherhood), DanTDM (Daniel Robert Middleton), Aphmau (Jessica Bravura) and LDShadowLady (Lizzie Dwyer) all made appearances as auction attendees for Steve's belongings. Mumbo Jumbo also helped design some of the movie's builds.

And of course, Mr. Minecraft himself Jens Bergensten, the Chief Creative Officer of Mojang Studios, made a brief cameo appearance as a waiter (serving Jennifer Coolidge on her date with the villager).

Did you know that *Steve's Lava Chicken* (the Jack Black 34-second ditty that Steve sings in the movie) broke into the UK Top 40 and Billboard Hot 100? Looks like Steve can officially add global popstar to his list of accolades.

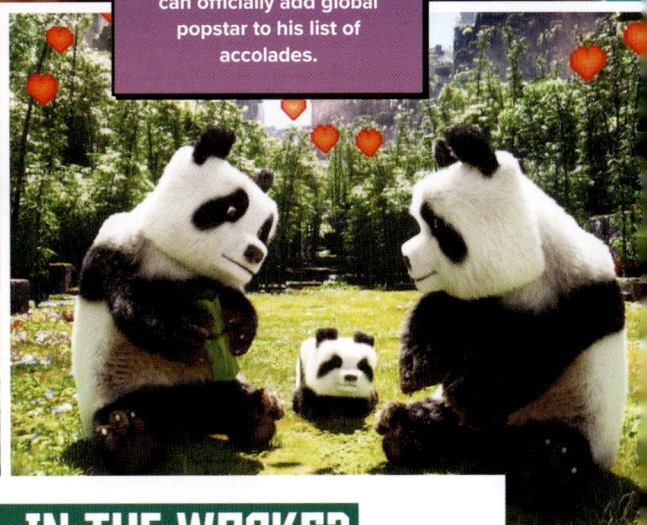

A SEQUEL IN THE WORKS?

Everyone knows by now that movies aren't over until the post-credits scene is done, so fans who watched to the very end saw Steve return to his old home... (wait for it)... to be greeted by a woman named...(keep waiting for it)... *Alex!*

THE END QUIZ

AFTER 60-OR-SO PAGES OF EVERYTHING MINECRAFT, IT'S FINALLY COME TO THIS: THE ULTIMATE TEST OF YOUR MINECRAFT MASTERY. ARE YOU READY TO PUT YOUR KNOWLEDGE TO THE TEST AND TAKE ON THE END QUIZ (JUST AS FEARSOME AND INTIMIDATING AS THE ENDER DRAGON, I ASSURE YOU)?
CHECK OUT P. 62-63 FOR ANSWERS.

VILLAGER

1. How long is one full day-night cycle IRL?

2. What is the rarest ore in the Overworld?

3. What do zombies drop when defeated?

4. Which biome can pandas be found in?

5. What do creepers drop when defeated?

ADVENTURER

6. Which mob shoots spit when provoked?

7. Which two structural blocks are affected by gravity?

8. What do you receive after slaying the Ender Dragon?

9. How many bookshelves are needed to unlock Lv 30 Enchantments?

10. Which hostile mob is immune to lava damage?

11. Which direction do sunflowers always face?

12. Which mob is the only hostile creature you can breed?

13. Which enchantment auto-collects nearby items?

14. Which mineral appears as ore in both the Overworld and the Nether?

15. Which food restores the most hunger saturation?

MAESTRO

16. What item is guaranteed in every Buried Treasure Chest?

17. What is the maximum fall distance a player can survive?

18. What is the chance of a baby zombie spawning?

19. What effect does a suspicious stew made with a poppy give?

20. Which block breaks the fastest with a hoe?

ANSWERS

22: FIND STEVE AND ALEX

42: ADVENTURER'S CROSSWORD

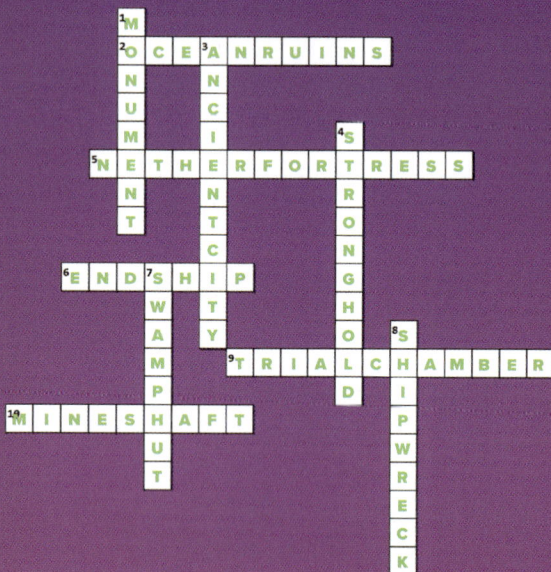

39: BLOCKSEARCH

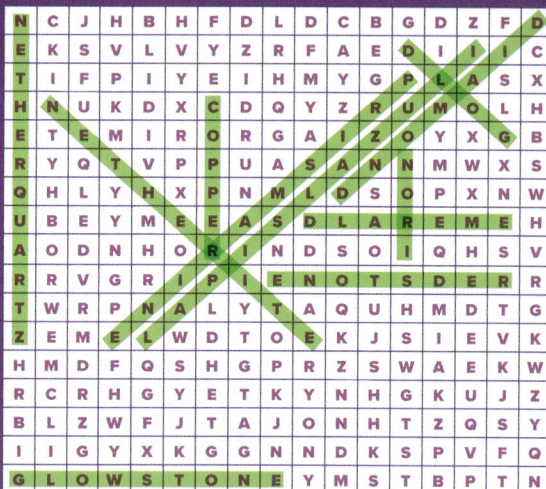

43: FRIENDLY MOBSEARCH

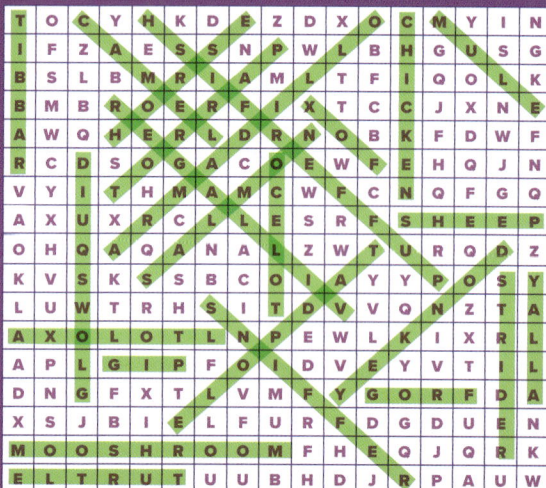

47: CRAFTING QUIZ

1. Chest
2. Flint and Steel
3. Bed
4. Bookshelf
5. Compass
6. Pickaxe
7. Fishing Rod
8. Bucket
9. Eye of Ender

50: SPOT THE DIFFERENCE